ALL-AMERICAN

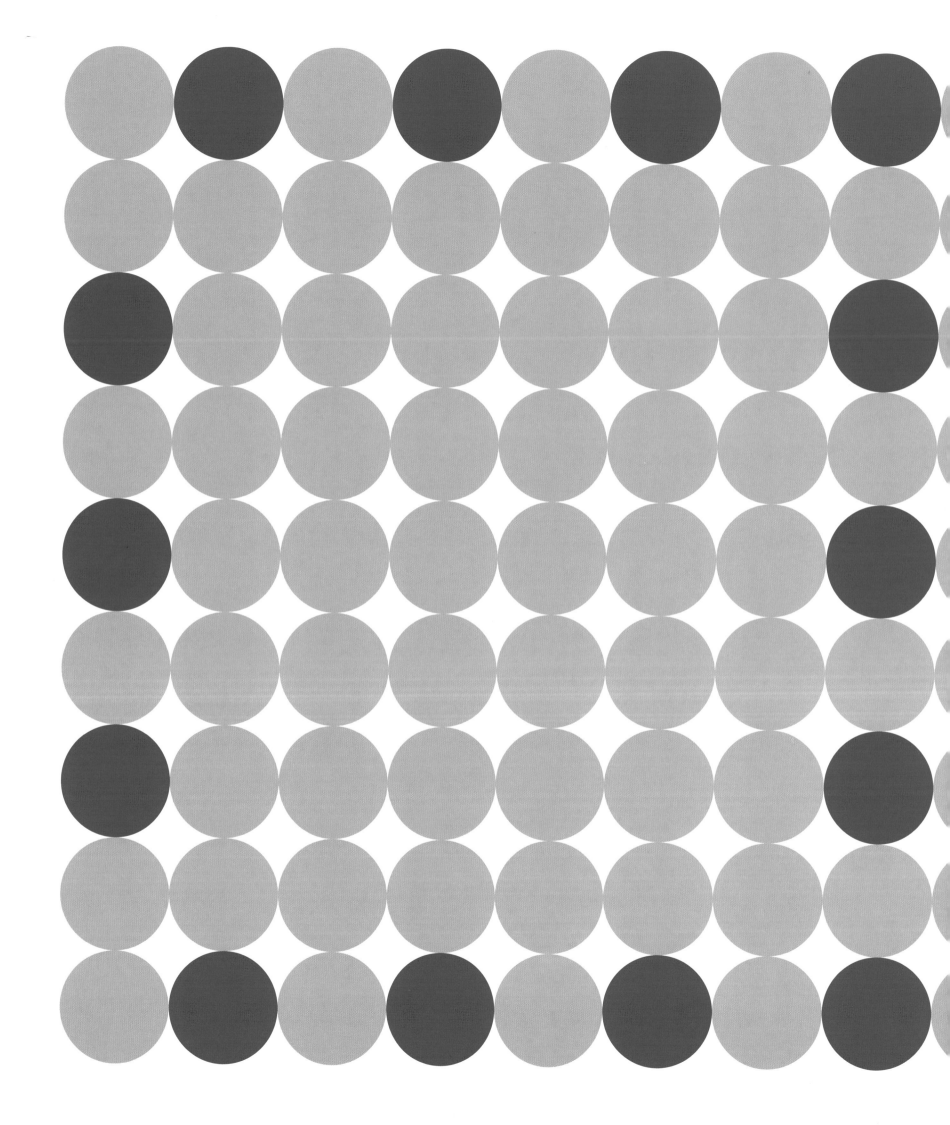

ALL-AMERICAN

THE EXUBERANT STYLE OF
WILLIAM DIAMOND AND ANTHONY BARATTA

PUBLISHER/EDITOR IN CHIEF: SUZANNE SLESIN
DESIGN: STAFFORD CLIFF
MANAGING EDITOR: JANE K. CREECH
PRODUCTION: DOMINICK SANTISE
TEXT: DAN SHAW
COPY EDITOR: ELIZABETH GALL

PHOTOGRAPHS BY MICHEL ARNAUD
POINTED LEAF PRESS, LLC.

Anthony Baratta

William Diamond

DUO

TRAD

FOLK

MOD

In 2005, Tony, left, and Bill were photographed on a pair of high-back wing chairs that had once been in the lobby of the Americana hotel in Miami, Florida. The designers had the pony-skin upholstery printed in a giraffe pattern. The chairs are now in Tony's Manhattan apartment.

William Diamond and Anthony Baratta are the decorating world's undisputed dynamic duo. Their legendary partnership (think Rodgers and Hammerstein, Nichols and May, or Batman and Robin) is unprecedented in a profession where star designers rarely want to share credit. But Bill and Tony are different. For nearly three decades they have collaborated on every project, including each other's houses. "We both expand each other's creativity enormously," Bill says. "If we separated right now, we would still be superb decorators, but we would never be what we are as a team."

While the pair is best known for its bold, graphic Pop Art approach to interiors, Bill and Tony work in many styles. They have decorated ski lodges, beach houses, townhouses, lofts, and penthouses and have rescued more than a few suburban McMansions from banality. Whether the clients want a modern, traditional, or country interior, Bill and Tony are never wishy-washy. They are always original, audacious, and sassy. Their rooms are comfortable, sumptuous, and joyful. They have redefined luxury in their own couture fashion. Diamond Baratta Design—as the partnership has been known since 1995—has refined a concept of luxury all about custom work and personalization. It's about designing a bedroom in a client's favorite colors and having one-of-a-kind fabrics, rugs, and linens made in the exact same hues to create a unique, harmonious space. It's about understanding a client's lifestyle and making sure the family room becomes a gathering place where every member of the family feels at home. It's about considering the geography and siting of a house or apartment and making sure the interior and exterior are in sync.

Work is fun for Bill and Tony because the creative process is the essence of their business. They go to museums to get inspiration for rugs from modern artists such as Jasper Johns, Frank Stella, and Cy Twombly. They will borrow a shape or line from a great painting and then blow it up, twist it, and tweak it, thereby creating a new pattern. They will recolor vintage fabrics in eye-popping combinations and resize them for a brand-new look and stunning impact. They reinvigorate classic fabrics—plaids, houndstooth, and argyles—by making them more emphatic and thus more exciting.

Bill and Tony thrive on brainstorming and profit from disagreeing. "We can go from A to Z with an idea in five minutes," Bill explains. "Tony will throw out an idea, and I'll say, 'No, no, no,' and suggest something else, and he'll say, 'No, no, no,' and the next thing you know, we have come up with an amazing solution." Tony concurs: "We allow ourselves to be edited. That we pass our ideas through each other is why it all works."

Every project is an opportunity for them to design original fabrics, furniture, rugs, and lighting fixtures. Some of those custom fabrics are now part of the Lee Jofa and Stark Carpet lines, while others are made only for each client and are not for commercial production. Every house or apartment inevitably has some flaw that requires them to change the architecture in order to create drama and elegance. Every day is a chance for them to dream up something new—reverse-painted glass doors to hide a refrigerator, or a braided rug in the shape of a target—and then hire artisans to fulfill their vision.

Bill and Tony met nearly thirty years ago in a curious fashion. Tony was working as a part-time office assistant to a psychiatrist Bill was seeing. When Bill complained that he was overworked, the therapist suggested that he hire Tony, who had just graduated from Fordham University with a degree in art history. Their first meeting was at the Museum of Modern Art, in New York, where Tony was working part-time: They toured the 1980 blockbuster Picasso show together (Tony secured the hard-to-get tickets) and discovered they had a shared sensibility. "I went to work for Bill as an apprentice," Tony says. "I was thinking about going to graduate school for architecture, but Bill told me that none of the architects he knew were very successful. He promised that I would do much better if I just worked for him."

Bill had been on a fast track since he had been bitten by the decorating bug on the eve of going to college. "When I was 17, I walked into decorator Pauline Feldman's house on Long Island—I was friends with her daughter—and I had an epiphany," he recalls. "I had never seen great decorating before, and this was *genius* decorating. I just stood there, studying it. I couldn't move. I had never been subjected before to *greatness*." (Bill and Pauline would later work together, and many of their projects were published in *House & Garden*.) When Bill arrived as a freshman at Carnegie Mellon University to study painting, he brought along his new fascination with design. "I started making huge paintings of interiors," he says. "At night I used to study architecture and decorating in the library because I had become *obsessed*."

Eventually, Bill transferred to New York's Pratt Institute and started working on his own, which led to his hiring Tony. "Tony was very quiet when he started working for me," Bill recalls. "I said, 'Tony, don't you understand that when you are a decorator, you have to have an opinion about *everything*—from the flowers and the tablecloths to the landscaping?' And he was the ultimate sponge. In about a year, he became a person who had opinions about everything."

Tony remembers how little he knew. "Bill and Pauline taught me everything about a certain way of living for a certain type of person," he says. "I come from suburban roots in New Jersey. I had to learn how to decorate for a world I wasn't accustomed to. I had to learn not one but many styles. At that time, they were interested in many styles—from Joseph Paul D'Urso's minimalism to Sister Parish's elegant traditionalism. But Bill and Pauline were interested only in the best. Bill would sit me down and we'd go through the magazines together, and he would tell me what he thought was good. You can't teach taste, but he taught me to be discerning."

As the business grew, Tony took charge of the architecture department, and when it became apparent how large his role was, Bill offered to make him his partner. "One of the reasons we work together so well is because we do the decorating and architecture at the same time," Tony says. "We find the flaws in each other's schemes. You learn by making mistakes, and we know that when you design a window, you should design the window treatment at the same time."

They have a deep respect for each other's perspective. "We are so yin and yang," Bill says. "One of the main reasons that we are amazing partners is that Tony is the only person in the world who can unstick me. We'll design a job, and I will become completely immersed in it and fall in love with it, and the client will come in and change twenty things about it and I'll get stuck. *But this was the perfect table!* Tony is never stuck, and he is open to everything."

After three decades, Tony remains in awe of Bill. "He always surprises me," Tony says. "His ideas are timeless. He comes up with the most exciting solutions over and over again. Bill is the master of furniture plans. He does things in clever ways. He pulls things that I would never expect out of a hat."

Bill and Tony don't claim to do this alone. When they brainstorm and spin out decorative fantasies, they always think of who they know who can execute their ideas. They have developed an extensive network of artisans and craftspeople whom they consider geniuses in their fields: Lois Chernin, an expert weaver and needlepointer; David Cohn, an artist who sketches designs for the handwoven rugs and paints beautiful murals; Kenneth DeAngelis, a master upholsterer; Paul Flammang, a talented furniture maker; Jan Jurta, who braids one-of-a-kind rugs; and Tom Newman, who crafts incredible tables.

Although Diamond Baratta Design's interiors are extremely photogenic, they were not created to be merely showplaces. They are the homes of people with the guts to commission furniture and rugs that don't come with recognizable labels attached to their undersides. They are the homes of people who are more interested in style than status. They are houses imbued with a spirit of optimism and joie de vivre. They are, counterintuitively, old-fashioned: After all, what's more classic than a comfortable home that feels like a personal haven? Yes, these are the houses of lucky and happy people.

Who are your design heroes?
Alberto Pinto, Robert Adam, John Fowler, Andrea Palladio, Dorothy Draper, Gio Ponti, Joseph Paul D'Urso, Sister Parish, Madeleine Castaing.

What is your favorite color?
Turquoise.

Where is the most colorful place you have ever been?
Colonia, Uruguay: It's the only place I have ever seen bougainvillea and hydrangea blooming profusely at the same time.

What do you consider exotic decorating?
The Chapel of the Rosary by Henri Matisse, Saint Paul de Vence in the South of France.

What do you consider safe decorating?
Traditional formulaic decoration, beige-and-white decorating, overplayed mid-century.

What is your favorite way to spend a Saturday afternoon?
Visiting historic homes: Philip Johnson's Glass House; Old Westbury Gardens; Kykuit, the Rockefeller Estate; Boscobel.

What's your favorite city?
Rome, for its incredible juxtaposition of ancient and modern. But there is nothing wrong with Paris.

What's your favorite building in New York? London? Paris?
New York: The Chrysler Building, the Guggenheim Museum.
Paris: The Louvre, L'institut du monde arabe by Jean Nouvel.
London: The Courtyard of the British Museum by Sir Norman Foster, Syon House and Osterley Park by Robert Adam.

What are your favorite places to shop in the United States?
New Orleans; Heart of the Country Antiques in Nashville, Tennessee; Antiques Week in Manchester, New Hampshire; Miami, Florida.

What are your favorite places to shop in Europe?
London, Stowe-on-the-Wold, Tetbury.

What's your most cherished possession?
I don't get attached to material possessions.

What do you collect?
Cars.

If you could own any painting in the world, what would it be?
Henri Matisse: The Red Studio.

Do movies influence your designs? Can you give examples?
Yes! The films of Ismail Merchant and James Ivory and the Hollywood movies of the thirties and forties.

Is style innate or can it be learned?
Innate.

What is the first thing you notice when you visit a house for the first time?
The style of the architecture, whether it has integrity, and whether the wings or additions are original.

What historic houses would you like to get your hands on?
La Villa Savoie by Le Corbusier, the Farnsworth House by Mies van der Rohe.

What is your dream project?
A home for a client who trusts us and is investing for the long term.

What do you like most about yourself?
My loyalty and honesty.

What do you dislike most about yourself?
My impatience.

Is it easier or harder to be a decorator today than it was twenty-five years ago? Explain.
Much harder, because the prices of all antiques keep going up and the quality keeps going down.

Who are your heroes in real life?
Pauline and Tony.

What do you consider your greatest achievement?
Learning to listen to people and give them what they want.

Who are your design heroes?
Le Corbusier; Sister Parish; Billy Baldwin; Michael Taylor; Dorothy Draper; the Adam brothers; McKim, Mead, and White; Gio Ponti; Jacques Emile Ruhlman.

What is your favorite color?
Red.

Where is the most colorful place you have ever been?
Vita Sackville-West's gardens in Sissinghurst, England.

What do you consider exotic decorating?
Anything with an Asian, African, or Middle Eastern influence.

What do you consider safe decorating?
Anything beige.

What is your favorite way to spend a Saturday afternoon?
At the Metropolitan Museum of Art in New York or on the beach in Miami, Florida.

What's your favorite city?
Miami.

What's your favorite building in New York? London? Paris?
New York: The United Nations Headquarters by Wallace K. Harrison.
London: The Courtyard of the British Museum by Sir Norman Foster.
Paris: L'institut du monde arabe by Jean Nouvel.

What are your favorite places to shop in the United States?
Los Angeles, New Orleans, Atlanta.

What are your favorite places to shop in Europe?
London.

What's your most cherished possession?
The bed made from two Victorian settees in my New York apartment.

What do you collect?
Plaster casts of classical sculpture, Victorian furniture, unusual seventies furniture.

If you could own any painting in the world, what would it be?
Andy Warhol's Gold Marilyn Monroe, 1962.

Do the movies influence your designs? Can you give examples?
Not generally, though I love watching early Busby Berkley and Fred Astaire movies.

Is style innate or can it be learned?
Innate.

What is the first thing you notice when you visit a house for the first time?
The light entering the house.

What historic houses would you like to get your hands on?
Kingsland Manor, the historic house a few blocks from my childhood home in Nutley, New Jersey.

What is your dream project?
My Cinema Paradiso fantasy, because I've always wanted to restore one of the grand movie theaters from the golden age.

What do you like most about yourself?
That most days I still come to work with a smile on my face.

What do you dislike most about yourself?
My obsessive personality.

Is it easier or harder to be a decorator today than it was twenty-five years ago? Explain.
Yes, it is harder. There's much more competition, since everybody thinks he or she can be a decorator. Also, with the development of cable television shows and Internet blogs, people seem to be into decorating as a career, but that doesn't always make for great decorating.

Who are your heroes in real life?
Doctors and research scientists working to rid the world of diseases.

What do you consider your greatest achievement?
Thirty years of keeping an office running in New York while feeling like our work is meaningful and new.

PREVIOUS PAGES Snapshots from Bill's early years have been set into Sunnyside, a print Diamond Baratta Design created for Lee Jofa. While growing up in Hewlett, New York, Bill was photographed in his grandfather's 1961 Lincoln, center, far left; in 1963 with his mother at summer camp, bottom, far left; as a bar mitzvah boy in 1965, the youngest of four generations, bottom, second from left; and with his mentor, Pauline Feldman, center, second from right.

LEFT Bill—who was photographed as a six-year-old with his maternal grandfather, Sidney Paul, in Stamford, Connecticut, while standing in a Chrysler 300 convertible—ascribes his love of cars to the fact that his grandfather always had three new models in his driveway at the same time. One, a four-door sedan, was for him; another, "Mother's car," was a coupe, though his wife did not have a driver's license; and the third was a convertible for his daughter, Dedee, who was not living at home. "He used all of them," Bill recalls. "He would get up and wash them every day. Grandpa was car-obsessed."

OPPOSITE In 1990, Bill posed in Southampton, New York, with his 1986 Porsche 911 convertible, one of his favorite cars.

OVERLEAF Three-year-old Tony tooled around in the front yard of his family's house in his hometown of Nutley, New Jersey, bottom, far left; at Racket Lake Camp in the mid-1980s, bottom row, second from left; graduating from college, center, with mortarboard; at his Communion, second row, third from left; and visiting Venice, Italy, third row, third from right. The fabric is Lee Jofa's Silhouettes by Diamond Baratta Design.

PREVIOUS PAGE LEFT "It's all about the bed and the sheets," Tony says. I love crawling into a glamorous bed with glamorous sheets." In the late 1990s, an ornate, upholstered, gilt headboard, a photograph of a plaster cast, and a crown hovering above a *T* all helped to create a Hollywood-like scene.

PREVIOUS PAGE RIGHT In Miami, Tony would often "hold court" in his bedroom, where New York artist Rob Wynne's wallpaper of giant butterflies created a dramatic backdrop behind the Victorian bed. A black-and-white Art Deco quilt and a pillow made from an Hermès beach towel completed the decor.

ABOVE Bill painted this eight-foot-long work of art in 1972, while he was a student at Carnegie Mellon University. His paintings—always imaginary rooms— were of interiors that "predated all we do: pattern-on-pattern and the mix of modern and traditional elements." Although he went to school to study painting, Bill was already obsessed with interior design.

ABOVE Tony set up guest quarters next door to his own apartment in Miami in 1999. The wild cacophony of patterns included a bedspread from Marimekko, a target rug, and wallpaper depicting high-school bullies by Philadelphia artist Virgil Marti. "The place was done in early Pop style," Tony says. "It was an exploration of the color-saturated, crazy world of the sixties."

ABOVE For a model room at 500 Park Avenue in Manhattan, Bill furnished a large, nearly all-glass living room with seating by the Finnish designer Alvar Aalto, which Bill had upholstered in a fabric hand-woven by Barbara Danenman. His inspiration came from the striped jersey worn by the *Peanuts* character Charlie Brown. In 1984, the use of strong color—red in this case—made Bill a maverick in the black-and-white world of minimalist design.

ABOVE When Tony decorated his Miami, Florida, apartment in the late 1990s, he used many pieces that had been kept in storage, including a pair of Victorian-style sofas that would later be made into the head- and footboard for a bed in his New York City apartment. "It was a strange mix of things," Tony admits. "It was black and white with intense tropical color."

OVERLEAF Shown is a selection of eighteen of the thirty-six covers of the most prominent home and interior design magazines in the United States and Europe that have featured projects by Diamond Baratta Design.

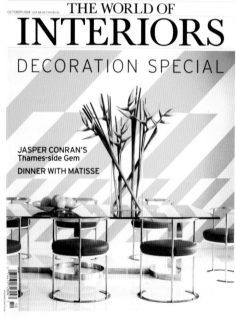

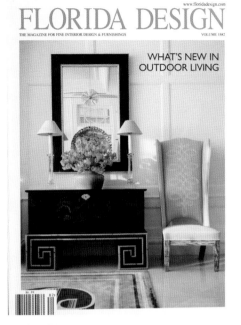

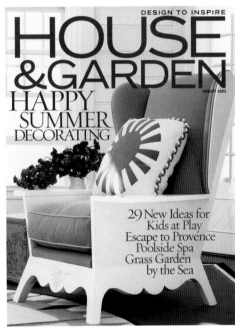

D U O

Their sensibilities could not be more different, yet they work together perfectly. Bill, far left, the more conservative one, let Tony help him transform his laid-back shingle-style cottage in East Hampton, New York, into a spirited, imaginative house where Early American veers toward American Pop. And Tony, left, with his brother Mark, returned the gesture by having Bill convince him to do his Florida apartment in bold citrus colors.

LEFT Red, white, and blue are favorite colors for many of the Diamond Baratta Design custom fabrics.

BILL *With me, it's all or nothing. And for eleven years I basically did very little to the country house I bought in East Hampton, New York, in 1998. I painted the walls, of course, put in central air-conditioning, and installed a new mahogany kitchen counter—but that was pretty much it. I didn't want to do too much (which is not my normal M.O.), because I loved that this was a genuine summer house without a basement or insulation and with original nineteenth-century glass in the windows. I loved that the walls were one board thick and that the same planks doubled as the downstairs ceiling and upstairs floors. I loved the location—walking distance to town and biking distance to the ocean—and how the house was sited in the corner of a half-acre parcel. This made the property seem expansive, and the setting was a surprise for a house so close to the historic village.*

The previous owner had divided the property into English-style garden "rooms." Uncharacteristically, I remained a passive observer of my land . . . until it grew out of control and I couldn't see the fingers in front of my face. I called landscape architect Perry Guillot, who has worked for many of my clients, and asked for his advice. He said that you can't have a mix of little and big trees when you live in town—you have to stick to one thing. So we removed eleven smaller trees and kept only the gorgeous, big, century-old ones. We also designed two new gardens with diamond-shaped boxwood parterres. (I have a weakness for visual puns, especially when it comes to my name.)

I wanted the house to be rustic and masculine, but I also wanted it to be fresh and have a dose of whimsy. I smile every time I arrive and see the black-and-white-painted floors, which are a cartoon version of wood grain and a nod to the needlepoint pillows of comic strip characters from my childhood. I commissioned David Cohn to create trompe l'oeil Adirondack-style paintings, which were my great indulgence. I had him give the paintings a three-dimensional quality, and they blow me away whenever I walk in the door. The only problem? If I ever decide to move, I can't take them with me (though I am sure Tony could think of a way for the walls to come with me, too). 🏠

OPPOSITE ABOVE Bill had the loggia's seven-foot-long table, which is generally used for summer lunches and dinners, made of lava stone in what he calls Ferrari Red. "It's the clearest primary," he says. The designer also had the floor painted in a black, gray, and white illusionistic box pattern.

OPPOSITE BELOW Vintage storage trunks that once held a lawyer's papers have been turned into coffee tables for the porch. All the furniture is covered in a graphic black-and-white-striped fabric. The painted signs came from an old tavern in New Hampshire; they reflect the swans that live nearby, in the picturesque pond that is a well-loved landmark of the seventeenth-century village of East Hampton.

RIGHT Tall, old trees providing both privacy and shade frame the traditional wood-shingled house that dates from 1810. Near the pool, a garden designed in a diamond pattern, in honor of the owner, has been planted with white roses and blue salvia and edged in boxwood. Although the covered porch is original to the house, the loggia was added about ten years ago and is now covered in dark green ivy.

RIGHT Comfortable chaise longues with black-and-white-striped pads are lined up by the pool, beside which bright red geraniums flourish in tubs. Towels are in the pattern of American flags.

LEFT In the shipshape galley kitchen, the one-and-a-quarter-inch-thick mahogany counters have been painted with deck enamel. The cabinet interiors are turquoise, to match the ceiling.

OPPOSITE The floors throughout the entryway, kitchen, and dining room have been painted black and decorated in a cartoon version of rough-hewn planking. Instead of using cushions for the dining room chairs, Bill had Jan Jurta of New Hampshire make targets in alternating turquoise and white braids.

OPPOSITE An antique Windsor bench is the focus of the foyer. For the floors, five artists under the direction of Adam Lowenbein were needed to paint the pastiche of wood-grained floorboards in a graphic white-over-black pattern. A large shutter, made in the same size as the off-center window, balances the wall and looks as though it were part of the original design. The vintage painted sign fits the space perfectly.

ABOVE LEFT AND ABOVE The narrow staircase is covered with a runner made of black and white braids, a modern accent to a traditional craft. The late-eighteenth-century yew chair was originally fitted with a chamber pot. The mahogany handrail was modeled on the traditional railings of ships and yachts.

LEFT AND OPPOSITE The inspiration for the dining room came from a photograph of painter Andrew Wyeth's house in Maine. "Mine is a version of his done by a decorator," says Bill, who wanted to create a contrast between the antique mahogany chairs, with their well-worn paint, and the bright white walls. Tony's design for the table was based on an eighteenth-century American example. Tom Newman, who makes many of Diamond Baratta Design's custom pieces, crafted it out of antique cherry. Bill collected the nineteenth-century dioramas—now set into the wall—in England, but in pursuit of perfectionism he repainted the yellowed sails white and turned the English flags into American ones. "They were not in perfect condition," Bill recalls. "And I could not stand the cracks, so I refurbished them."

OVERLEAF The custom-colored tartan fabric that Bill asked Lois Chernin of Oswego, New York, to weave for him is the star of the living room. Tony had the two tall cabinets, which Bill bought in London twelve years ago, raised two feet so that they would reach above the French doors and be in better proportion to the room. The red, turquoise, black, and white color scheme of the house is reproduced in the designs of the needlepoint throw pillows Chernin crafted. They were drawn by Lowenbein to represent artwork that Bill loved as a boy. "Tony hated them," Bill admits, "but it was just something I had to do."

ABOVE A needlepoint Dagwood pillow is a perfect match for a shelf full of *National Geographic* magazines and a vintage painted tin car.

ABOVE Sixty-two photographs of forty-foot sailboats, taken in 1929 by Edwin Levick, have been placed in identical mahogany frames painted in the same warm colors as the images. The lamp base is made from an antique ship's buoy. The red-and-white Tarrant Plaid is by Diamond Baratta Design for Lee Jofa.

OPPOSITE The space over the mantel-piece needed what Bill calls "something major." He found it in an evocative photograph by David Knox of two derelict but charming buildings. "Some people think it's this house, but it's so not my house!" says Bill, who took the liberty of switching the position of the two houses so that the more pristine one was at eye level.

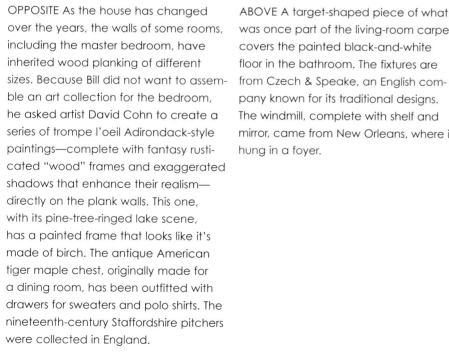

OPPOSITE As the house has changed over the years, the walls of some rooms, including the master bedroom, have inherited wood planking of different sizes. Because Bill did not want to assemble an art collection for the bedroom, he asked artist David Cohn to create a series of trompe l'oeil Adirondack-style paintings—complete with fantasy rusticated "wood" frames and exaggerated shadows that enhance their realism—directly on the plank walls. This one, with its pine-tree-ringed lake scene, has a painted frame that looks like it's made of birch. The antique American tiger maple chest, originally made for a dining room, has been outfitted with drawers for sweaters and polo shirts. The nineteenth-century Staffordshire pitchers were collected in England.

ABOVE A target-shaped piece of what was once part of the living-room carpet covers the painted black-and-white floor in the bathroom. The fixtures are from Czech & Speake, an English company known for its traditional designs. The windmill, complete with shelf and mirror, came from New Orleans, where it hung in a foyer.

ABOVE Because there are very few closets in the house, clothes are hung on pegs. The paintings, including the three-dimensional-looking fish diorama, are by David Cohn.

ABOVE David Cohn also painted the rustic scenes that surround the bed. Each has illusionistic shadows that would be cast by the frames if they were three-dimensional.

RIGHT The painted cottage-style bed, with a majestic stag portrayed on the headboard, was enlarged from its original width of forty-five inches to that of a queen-size bed. Craftsman Kevin Cross added the canopy and the columns on the head- and footboards. The handwoven red-and-white-checked fabric is trimmed in a wide tape.

TONY *Ten years ago, I bought a small apartment in the South Beach section of Miami, Florida, to use as a winter get-away. I stayed there often, and when I decided that I should upgrade to an apartment with views of the water, I found a clean-lined, one-bedroom duplex with unobstructed views of turquoise Biscayne Bay. The duplex had been recently reno-vated, so I wouldn't have to do any work. "It's in move-in condition," I told Bill when I showed him some photographs. "Are you kidding?" he replied.*

Bill was right, and the only item I ended up bringing from my previous apartment was the Art Deco letter A that now hangs on the wall over my bed. I wanted this place to have a color scheme different from anyplace I had lived before. So I decided on orange, yellow, and white. I also decided I would not have any black in the apartment, which meant painting all the window frames. And I wanted to use new materials: for instance, on the floors and bathroom walls, a Chinese glass that looks like marble; for the bedroom, a wet-look wallpaper. The many shiny and reflective surfaces in this apartment can, I confess, be a drag if you're someone who likes to keep things spotless. I am always with the Windex.

Although it was not my original intention to give this apartment a 1970s tone (I wanted the place to feel modern, not retro), I fell in love with a couple of pieces of furniture that set the course: a molded plastic desk by Maurice Calka and a vintage Milo Baughman chaise longue. I love this chair: It's a cross between an amusement park ride and something that would be on the starship U.S.S. Enterprise. I bought the chaise for watching television, but I can sit on it and look in any direction because the chair pivots. It's a great perch for watching the sunsets, which are absolutely spectacular here. The view is nonstop, 24/7, and it never fails to astonish and entertain me. It's the most beautiful part of my home. 🏠

PREVIOUS PAGES The wide-open view convinced Tony that the duplex in one of Miami's classic apartment buildings was the one for him. A shopping trip to London helped him move toward a reinterpretation of the 1970s—with a style that retains its own distinct character. The vintage rocking chaise longue, by Milo Baughman, a well-known American mid-century designer, was re-covered in a lemon yellow synthetic canvas.

ABOVE Luigi Caccia Dominioni, the Milanese architect, designed the chairs surrounding the Tobia Scarpa table in the dining area in 1958. The glass top was made as large as could fit into the building's elevator.

OPPOSITE One of French sculptor Maurice Calka's most famous works is the crayon yellow molded-fiberglass boomerang desk he produced as a limited edition for Leleu-Deshays in 1969. Tony found the desk through Joel Chen, a Los Angeles dealer. The desk chair is by Arne Jacobsen; the 1970s sculpture, by an unknown artist. To get the late-sixties, early-seventies wet look he wanted for the room's walls, Tony applied bright orange vinyl wallpaper from Stark.

RIGHT The huge sofa in the living room is an invention modeled on seating that Tony remembered from old photographs. Wide leather belts made especially for the sofa trim the bolsters. The pillows and side chairs are covered in a fabric whose pattern of intersecting little pills, by Diamond Baratta Design, was inspired by the work of Damien Hirst, the celebrated English artist. The set of framed ink-drip paintings is by Ceal Floyer, a Pakistan-born artist. Italian architect Cini Boeri designed the glass and chrome coffee table for Knoll. Its off-center oval base reflects the brightly colored bull's-eye rug that was made by Stark Carpet.

OVERLEAF Because Tony had always wanted a mural in his home, he commissioned the artist Adam Lowenbein to create a dynamic piece incorporating the new yellow-and-white color scheme based on a small drawing he had seen by Alexander Girard, the American designer particularly known for his textiles.

ABOVE AND ABOVE RIGHT The stairs that link the bedroom on the lower level to the living room above are made of white glass, extending the reflective surfaces of the duplex. Looking up, one catches a glimpse of the dining-area mural; looking down toward the bedroom offers a glimmer of a classic pond yacht that Tony brought back from England and that happens to coordinate with the overall color scheme.

OPPOSITE The master bathroom is entirely lined in white glass and outfitted with a pair of sinks topped by two slim medicine cabinets. Under-the-counter plumbing is hidden behind a frosted glass panel.

LEFT A Damien Hirst print, one of a pair, frames the bed in the master bedroom. The headboard of upholstered white leather circles edged in orange piping takes its cues from the Marshmallow sofa designed by George Nelson and Irving Harper and introduced by the Herman Miller Furniture Company in 1956. "I love a very striking bed," Tony says. "That's part of my signature." The bedcover is a Diamond Baratta Design pattern called Chopin, because it is made up of two inverted pianos. Another typical Tony touch is the 1970s-style monogram on the pillow. The Art Deco letter A, powder-coated in white, is the only item the designer brought from his former apartment.

OPPOSITE The oval bedside tables are based on a design by Guiseppe Terragni, an Italian architect who worked in the 1930s. The multicolored rug by Stark Carpet was inspired by the work of English contemporary artist Bridget Riley.

TRAD

Hand-carved moldings, silk draperies, and marquetry floors are hallmarks of traditional decorating. With a nod to the timeless qualities of a grand style, Bill and Tony transpose these elements in a bold but more informal manner. By selecting rich, clear colors, reconfiguring classic patterns, and reinventing remarkable furniture designs with a new vision and scale, the two metamorphose tradition into a spirited, contemporary style of living for today.

LEFT On this rendering, Bill selected the eighty-five colors needed for the custom-made rug by Stark Carpet.

OLD WORLD *We had known the clients who own this huge old house in Connecticut for years before they asked us to consult on their already-in-progress renovation. She really loves our decorating style and has followed our work for a long time. That is always very flattering. She is into every microscopic aspect of decorating, so everything in her home must have the right trim, the right contrasting braid, and she doesn't stop until it's perfect. Furthermore, she has exquisite taste but is not afraid to take chances—or even make mistakes. When one is made, she does it over until it's right. That explains why we were able to create amazing things in this house. For example, our client remembered seeing old English chintzes and allowed us to commission fabric houses to reprint some of their fabulous yet no longer available designs. These beautiful fabrics—which we used to upholster chairs and sofas in the living room, master bedroom, family room, and the lovely sitting room overlooking the garden—are wonderful and unique.*

For the extraordinary two-story kitchen, we showed her a sketch with a big clock, and then off we went! The couple started out with a quite normal house and ended up with anything but one. 🏠

PREVIOUS PAGES The 1920s Colonial Revival house has a colonnaded porch, added by Diamond Baratta Design, that creates a gracious entrance. The swimming pool has been integrated into the estate-like garden overlooking the lake.

LEFT The six-foot-high brass hanging lantern was designed by Tony and custom-made in London. New paneling was installed to act as a backdrop for a collection of horse paintings. The spindles on the staircase were inspired by the work of McKim, Mead, and White, an architectural firm that was prominent at the beginning of the twentieth century.

OPPOSITE The large scale of the double-height foyer elicited a dramatic response from the designers, who had the floor stained in a faux-marquetry geometric pattern of large compasses. Diamond Baratta Design created the center table in tiger maple, basing it on an antique rent table with pullout drawers. Kevin Cross made the overscale versions of the eighteenth-century Hepplewhite chairs.

OPPOSITE The elaborate rosette and tassel are quirky details of the sofa arm.

RIGHT AND BELOW RIGHT The walls of the large living room, an updated version of old-school decorating, have been painted an extraordinary hue—the color of Granny Smith apples—rendered in a crosshatch lacquer glaze. Because the client wanted to use traditional old English chintzes that were no longer in production, the designers had 150 yards of some of the most extraordinary patterns rescreened. Here they are used on the sofa and easy chairs. Luxurious inch-thick sisal has been made into a wall-to-wall floor covering. The white moldings, overdoors, and ceiling give the room a fresh jolt.

OVERLEAF The formal dining room, carved out of what was once the gentlemen's smoking room and the ladies' dressing room, is defined by its painted oval floor. The chairs are English antiques, and the chandelier is French and from the early nineteenth century. Another special detail includes the seat covers, which were embroidered with the client's monogram. The lovely draperies have pinkish-red silk peeking through green silk. They are trimmed in oversize handmade Scalamandré tassels. The bucolic mural was specially painted for the room by the Kevin Cross Studio. A collection of blue-and-white Staffordshire china fills the oval glass cabinets.

LEFT AND OPPOSITE A rug made up of round and diamond shapes connected with braiding is the star in the family room, once the house's dining room. Favorite dogs, the daughter of the house on horseback, and summer strawberries are some of the motifs depicted. Tony first cut off the column of a stone capital to make the coffee table and then topped it with a piece of *verre églomisé*—reverse-painted glass with gold leaf and stars by Miriam Ellner. The large-strawberry-decorated fabric is a reproduced, recolored design by D.D. and Leslie Tillett, who were well known in the 1960s for their hand-printed fabrics.

OPPOSITE In the style of famed American decorator Dorothy Draper, a lighting fixture in the shape of a tole birdcage, covered in ivy, hangs from the dome of the trellised room.

ABOVE Craftsman Paul Flammang created an elaborate trellis with complex curves for the room off the master bedroom that overlooks the grounds.

ABOVE The sunny French-windowed space off the living room has been dubbed the Versailles Room because of its delicate, antique-looking moldings, which were already in place when the clients moved in. The carved wood chandelier and the floral chintz, reproduced from an old Clarence House design, are sophisticated country elements. The custom-made, hand-needlepointed rug by Stark Carpet has a pattern of delft tiles in green, yellow, and white. The armchair is an antique from the famous English firm of Colefax and Fowler. Because the room is sometimes used as the man of the house's home office, his monogram has been embroidered in oval cameos on a fleur de lys lace on the demi-lune windows.

OVERLEAF The master bathroom—with its sixteen-foot ceilings, a tub from Urban Archaeology made out of one piece of marble, and a double shower installed in a gazebo—is luxurious and relaxing. The English mossy green walls blend in with the pale blue ceiling. The painting is by Jacqueline Marval, a French artist who worked at the beginning of the last century.

ABOVE The shower in the master bathroom is ensconsed in an eleven-foot-high domed gazebo covered in wood trelliswork. The interior is made entirely of marble slabs.

ABOVE The Venetian mirror over one of the matching vanities covers a medicine cabinet. A trellis pattern also decorates the marble-topped cabinet.

ABOVE On the landing near the master bedroom, an antique settee has been upholstered in an appliquéd quilt fabric, edged with a scalloped border by artist Erin Wilson.

ABOVE Tony had a "glamorous twenties fantasy" in mind for the master bedroom: He added the curved architectural elements and placed an antique Venetian mirror over the mantelpiece. The overscale, tufted club chairs are a Diamond Baratta Design invention based on a Victorian antique. The headrests and scroll-sided mahogany footstools are new additions.

RIGHT The eighteen-foot-high ceilings and a Palladian window set the tone for the grandiose eat-in kitchen designed around those in eighteenth-century English country houses. Everything in the room—from the enormous hood over the French La Cornue stove to the marble-topped island and tall glass-fronted cabinets—was specially made for this kitchen.

ABOVE A new Sub-Zero refrigerator is hidden behind doors that recall turn-of-the-twentieth-century icebox units. Its hardware has been newly cast from old models.

ABOVE The fantastical overdoor that came from the entrance of the house now serves as a highly original mantelpiece. Vintage delft tiles line the fireplace.

ABOVE Woodwork and moldings were custom-made to include a large antique clock. The marble counters and island are functional *and* good-looking, which allows the room to be used for entertaining.

ABOVE Because of the scale of the ten-foot-high Palladian window, the designers devised a hand-turned urn, made by Paul Flammang, to house the custom-made P.E. Guerin faucet.

NEOCLASSIC *Located in Darien, Connecticut, this gracious, generously scaled Colonial Revival house has been attributed to the New York architectural firm McKim, Mead, and White. Although the exterior has been left untouched, the home needed interiors that would be elegant but not stuffy in any way and could accommodate the needs of a young family. We emphasized the house's beautiful lines and chose pretty colors and old-world furnishings—such as hand-printed wallpaper and antique Chippendale chairs—to bring it into this century.* 🏠

RIGHT Because the house is built on a steep grade, six steps lead from the front door to the main level. A set of plaster plaques in the style of Wedgwood china line the vestibule. The seats of the beautiful Chinese Chippendale chairs are upholstered in a green-striped, embossed velvet fabric.

LEFT A Waterford crystal chandelier hangs in the formal dining room, where chairs that have been in the client's family for years have been updated with skirted seats in a green-and-chartreuse gingham fabric.

OPPOSITE The antique faience rose urns were replicated on the hand-painted Chinese wallpaper commissioned from Gracie Inc. in New York.

LEFT The stair runner at Boscobel, the nineteenth-century neoclassical mansion overlooking the Hudson River in upstate New York, inspired the design of the striped runner on the staircase leading from the entrance foyer to the second floor. Here the carpeting has been recolored and tripled in size by Scalamandré. An Empire chaise sits on the half landing. The floor has been painted in a geometric pattern derived from stylistic elements in the work of the neoclassical English architect Robert Adam.

OPPOSITE The skylighted greenhouse room has a mix of furniture that includes an Empire settee and metal garden pieces from the 1940s. The rug, by Diamond Baratta Design, is made up of a pattern of Chinese fretwork and flowers and was specially fabricated for this room by Stark Carpet. Gingham wallpaper shades and a wire chandelier add jaunty touches to the room.

BESPOKE *This is very much a gentleman's house, and every inch of it is handsome. The space was a blank canvas—a completely gutted brick townhouse in Manhattan—that one of our longtime clients bought when he became a bachelor again. Luckily, we knew his taste so well that we could communicate in shorthand when discussing moldings, fabrics, and furniture. We were quite familiar with our client's horse paintings by Sir Alfred Munnings (who gained fame for the equestrian portraits he made for the British royal family), and we understood that the decor needed to compliment those pictures as well as our client's collection of golf paintings.*

The step-down entry foyer posed the greatest challenge, because we had to figure out how to deal with the counterintuitive notion of walking down steps as you enter. We ended up building settles by the front door and connecting them to a sweeping balustrade, which creates a sense of occasion when guests arrive. The client wanted a clubby living room, so we had exquisite paneling made in England of Baltic pine, which has a warm antique feel unlike anything available in the United States.

By the time the house was finished, we learned that the client had a new woman in his life, and we wondered whether she would demand changes to the decor. Happily, the house fit her like a glove—it's the perfect environment for a person with her impeccable style. Indeed, the couple decided to have their wedding in the house, and as we watched her greet the guests in the foyer, we thought we had never seen a woman who looked so much at home. 🏠

OPPOSITE New planters and a door painted peacock blue are recent touches added to the facade of the 1920s Colonial Revival townhouse located on a lovely side street on Manhattan's Upper East Side.

RIGHT The fireplace in the entrance hall is lined with delft tiles. Mahogany carvings were added to the new mantelpiece, to add heft to the space.

OVERLEAF The interior architecture of the foyer was reconfigured to include two wing chair–like benches (reminiscent of the church pews Tony recalled from his Catholic childhood). Outlined in mahogany, they accentuate the clean white woodwork.

LEFT The handsome dining room (the client was a bachelor when the house was being decorated) has walls done in a peacock blue color with a masculine cross-hatch pattern. The fabric on the chairs is Bill's fanciful interpretation of glen plaid. An enormous silver-plated chandelier, a reproduction of an eighteenth-century fixture, is centered over the Georgian-style table made by craftsman Tom Newman. Eighteenth-century delft platters coordinate with the delft vases used as lamp bases. The nineteenth-century equestrian painting is by Sir Alfred Munnings, one of England's finest painters of horses.

OPPOSITE Since the client favors only English pine, the paneling in the sitting room was crafted in London and shipped to New York. The eighteenth-century painting is a portrait of a man who was a doctor and golfer. The coffee table, by Diamond Baratta Design, was inspired by English Regency furniture. The wing chair is a reproduction of one of the designers' favorite models; the side chair is an antique bought at auction. The lamp base was made from an antique delft jar.

CLUBBY *Creativity often benefits from constraints, and that is certainly the case when decorating a jet. For such a design, safety is paramount and* everything *must be approved by the Federal Aviation Administration.*

We knew the plane's owner quite well from designing two houses for him, so we had a good sense of what would suit his personality. Remembering how much he loves to sail, we decided the interior of the fourteen-seat Gulfstream 400 should resemble a yacht's. So we paneled the walls in the most beautiful etimoe, *a hardwood with a very luxurious 1930s quality. The* floors in the galley are varnished holly and mahogany, which are also used in boats. We put down a tartan carpet in the main cabin and upholstered the seats in butter-soft leather with luggage stitching. We even chose the china and the flatware, to ensure that every design element complemented the others. There's just one word that comes to mind when we think about this sporty, masculine jet, but it's a word that sophisticated folks are not supposed to use. Nevertheless, we're going to break the rule: We think this plane is* classy.

OPPOSITE, ABOVE LEFT, AND ABOVE
Although the exterior of the fourteen-seat Gulfstream 400 is sleek and exudes twenty-first-century sophistication, its perfectly appointed interior, including the wood-lined galley, has a traditional aura that harks back to early aviation.

RIGHT The airplane's interior is lined with highly polished mahogany-like *etimoe*. Seats are upholstered in soft leather, and custom-designed plaid carpeting covers the floor. The oval windows are trimmed in nickel to look like portholes and help carry through the yacht imagery. The accessories are from Hermès.

FOLK

All houses have stories, but there's something particularly appealing about the tales told when rooms are filled with antique game boards and weather vanes, and carpets in which new versions of Early American prints spring to life. Fabrics woven with the initials of family members, rugs that depict pets and hobbies, and other perfectly crafted details—floors painted with summer fruits or lovely scenic murals—all help to redefine the charm of folk art.

LEFT Wilderness scenes in rustic frames by David Cohn are the basic elements for a custom-woven rug.

AMERICANA *These Connecticut clients discovered us when they saw our 2006 book,* Diamond Baratta Design, *which they used like a workbook to show us what they had in mind for this project. They are a very fun couple with a blended family that resembles a modern-day* Brady Bunch, *and they wanted their home to combine a sense of collective history with an "anything goes" attitude.*

If you were to mistake the raised-panel foyer for the living room, you would be forgiven: The proportions of this shingle and stone house are beyond generous. On shopping trips with the clients to England and New Hampshire, we purchased a marvelous mix of antique furniture including American, English, French, and Swedish pieces that work together well because they all share a country house aesthetic that transcends time and place.

Our client is a serious collector with a great eye—every one of the weather vanes displayed in the foyer is best-in-class— and she and her husband also appreciate and support contemporary craftsmen. They hired a muralist to paint the dining room walls with scenes portraying their town in earlier times. For a wing chair in the family room, the two enthusiastically endorsed our idea of having a custom Scottish ingrain fabric made to incorporate the initials of all their children. And because we wanted to add a layer of whimsy and personality to a quite handsome kitchen, we painted the floor with a watermelon-and-strawberry pattern and commissioned the stained-glass artist Patrick Clark to design panels that could be inserted into the smaller cabinet doors. These stained-glass fruits and farm animals are not just decorative—they are also modern folk art of the highest order. 🏠

RIGHT The raised-paneled foyer was the perfect backdrop for an enviable collection of antique weather vanes, which the designers decided to hang on the wall with specially made brackets. The large eighteenth-century Swedish settee in the front hall has been upholstered in a custom ingrain fabric depicting houses in a landscape. The unusual twenty-two-inch-high pitchers are English transferware.

OPPOSITE The rug in the foyer, based on a scene in a nineteenth-century American print, depicts the charm of riding in a horse-drawn carriage. It was crafted in a combination of Aubusson-style embroidery and tufting by Stark Carpet.

RIGHT A glorious leafy tree is rendered in a three-dimensional mode on the rug in the living room.

OPPOSITE AND ABOVE Early American
engravings of children playing in a
bucolic landscape were the inspiration
for the extraordinary rug in the living
room, where French and Italian furnishings are mixed in an original way. Four
antique Italian overdoors of painted still
lifes are hung above the sofa covered
in a historic document print fabric from
Pierre Deux.

RIGHT A glass trapezoid-shaped former shop fixture, electrified and fitted with silk lamp shades, has been transformed into a dramatic lantern in the romantic dining room. Four of the chairs are eighteenth-century Portuguese antiques; eight are line-for-line reproductions. The rug, designed for the room, is patterned in botanically correct bouquets of blue flowers and was specially woven by Stark Carpet. The artist Andrew Tedesco painted the mural depicting charming eighteenth-century scenes in a Connecticut town in the manner of Currier and Ives. The drapery fabric, originally a multicolored textile from the English manufacturer Geoffrey Bennison, has been recolored in blue and white.

OPPOSITE The large mahogany-armed wing chair by Diamond Baratta Design has been covered in a complex woven fabric that incorporates the first initial of each of the six children in the family along with intricate designs of weather vanes and game boards.

ABOVE The existing stone fireplace in the family room was a key to the cozy Adirondack-lodge look the clients desired. The large clock originally hung in a train station. The furnishings have a rustic feeling: The sofa is covered in New London Plaid, produced by Lee Jofa and created by Diamond Baratta Design with a lot of yellow to give the room some added punch. A star-quilt pattern is the central motif of the rug, which ties the room together. A garland of flowers was added because the client likes pretty things.

LEFT Hand-blocked American document wallpaper from Adelphi Paper Hangings has been used on the landing of the upstairs hallway, where an early-nineteenth-century setback cabinet is filled with a collection of nineteenth-century English strawberryware.

OPPOSITE The painted floor, with its pattern of strawberries and watermelons on a blue-and-white checkerboard, stars in the warm, welcoming kitchen. The two islands have countertops of bright red lava stone, and the wall behind the restaurant-style stove has been covered with eighteenth-century blue-and-white Portuguese tiles. Patrick Clark made the fruit-motif stained-glass panels that have been set into the cabinet doors. The ceiling is covered with a red-and-white gingham wallpaper by Diamond Baratta Design, which softens the look of the spec-built house.

COUNTRY *Many of our clients call us when they are in the middle of building a house and realize that we might have some thoughts on the layout and finishes. We arrived at this house in the Berkshires, in Massachusetts, when the framing was going up. The architect had designed a bridge spanning the living room to connect the two wings of the house. We told our clients that we would not work on the house as long as a bridge was cutting the living room in half. The clients were stunned. We would not negotiate, and we were trusted to design two handsome matching staircases to reach the second floor.*

Because the living room's two fireplaces were part of the architect's original design, our double staircase is in harmony with the big, barnlike room. The millwork on the banisters, paneling, and mantels, based on historic nineteenth-century styles, creates a unified, classic backdrop for a new collection of folk art. A pair of custom-tartan-upholstered wing chairs flanks each fireplace, and the sofas are covered in a graphic weather vane print. The look is both tailored and exuberant.

One of the challenges with traditional-style new construction is giving a home a sense of a pedigree. The dining room was quite lackluster for a house of its size and quality, though the windows offered an awesome view. We reproduced eighteenth-century-style paneling from drawings we found in a Works Progress Administration book to cover only the lower three-quarters of the wall, which allowed room for a wrap-around mural of the local New England village during the Revolutionary era. For the kitchen, we had the pantry doors made of sheets of perforated tin, like those found on antique pie safes. The doors are a contemporary folk art piece and one of our all-time favorite kitchen innovations. 🏠

LEFT An antique weather vane and a vintage barber pole hang near the stairs.

OPPOSITE Once the overhead gallery was replaced by twin stairs with beautifully executed nineteenth-century-style woodwork detailing, the living room could be furnished symmetrically. The large sofa, one of a pair, is covered in a print with weather vanes by Diamond Baratta Design.

RIGHT The hooked and braided rug custom-designed for the living room incorporates round vignettes, each encircled in braid, that relate to the Lenox, Massachusetts, farm scenery. Hooked Pennsylvania hex signs fill in the pattern. The wing chairs are covered in a custom-woven plaid.

FAR LEFT AND LEFT Spectacular antique quilts—one an album quilt, the other a star quilt—hang like paintings over the two facing fireplaces in the living room. A pair of plaid-covered wing chairs flanks each mantelpiece.

BELOW FAR LEFT An antique hatmaker's insignia stands near a table lamp whose base is made from a vintage milk jug.

BELOW LEFT Each of the circles in the rug depicts a different scene in the bucolic surroundings.

OPPOSITE The fireplace surrounds are made from a series of ceramic reproduction-delft tiles. The cast-iron andirons, in the shape of Hessian soldiers, match the fireplace tools.

LEFT In the master bedroom, a period American Federal wing chair has been upholstered in white matelassé and adorned with a swag of brass nail heads that continue along the graceful curve of the arms. Bill designed the tartan rug, hand-woven by Stark Carpet, predominantly in yellow and white with a touch of red.

OPPOSITE The room's elegant palette is pale and subdued. An antique game board's checkered pattern echoes the yellow and white tiles of the fireplace surround.

LEFT Instead of fitting glass panels into the doors of the huge pantry cabinet in the kitchen, the designers created a series of patterns that were punched out of tin panels in the manner of old pie safes. The initial of the clients' last name was also punched out, in the panel at the top right.

RIGHT The red-and-white-checkerboard backsplash gives the kitchen a fresh, high-spirited look. Rounded cabinets and a series of six English lanterns provide extra interest.

OPPOSITE, ABOVE, AND ABOVE RIGHT
Because the sitting room off the master
bedroom has a row of small windows
admitting very little natural light, the
designers decided to keep the space on
the dark side. The walls are covered in
red felt, and the furniture is upholstered
with a handwoven red-and-white plaid.
In keeping with the folk art feeling of
the house, the rug has an abstracted
pattern of hex signs. Shutters were
added to the windows, and shelves are
filled with a collection of old firkins. The
tall cabinet is a French-Canadian piece
that came from Monique Shay Antiques
in Woodbury, Connecticut.

LEFT AND OPPOSITE The original dining room was lackluster, so Tony designed a version of eighteenth-century American paneling and created a firebox to better balance the fireplace wall. Above the paneling, Ilya Shevel painted the mural depicting the town of Lenox, Massachusetts, near where the house is located. A collection of blue Staffordshire platters offers a decorative touch. The rug, woven by Stark Carpet, was inspired by eighteenth-century American felt work and includes a variety of animal and floral motifs. A red wing chair is placed at the head of the table to contrast with the more rustic Windsor side chairs. The backs of the chairs are covered with exquisite needlepoint antimacassars.

PREVIOUS PAGES Dramatic mountains, wide-open skies, and tall pines are all part of the awe-inspiring Idaho land-scape that can be seen from the house. The sheer expanse of the views seemed to decree that the decorating be bold.

ABOVE LEFT AND ABOVE "This was not a typical Western interior: It was, rather, a bit campy and tongue-in-cheek on pur-pose for a family who could handle it," Tony explains. Any wall that was not load-bearing—in this case, not made of logs—was covered in either wood planks or fabric. The foyer wall that rises to the second floor was upholstered with a computer-generated pattern, in reds and dark green, of a traditional quilt by Jaime Magoon, an associate at Diamond Baratta Design. The eleven-foot-high cowboy sign was one of the clients' finds.

RUSTIC *When it comes to decoration, most log cabins in the Rocky Mountains are the strong, silent type. Our clients did not want their lodge outside of Sun Valley, Idaho, to be wishy-washy Western. They wanted something fantastical (but practical, too, because they have three school-age daughters), and they trusted us because we had already decorated their home in Connecticut and helped them start a collection of folk art.*

We've always maintained that there is a strong link between folk art and Pop Art, and we get jazzed by inventing hybrids such as the patchwork sofa cushions inspired by the seminal paintings of Robert Indiana. We love to buy antique pieces, but because there is a serious shortage of great folk art on the market we often create our own accessories and decorative objects. This allows us to get the exact sizes and colors we want for a particular project. We are always excited when we hire artisans to make things such as the totem poles carved by hand in Minnesota, the Adirondack Great Camp–style twig bed (which auction houses will be fighting over someday), and the scenic panels for the rustic doors leading to the linen and water closets in the girls' bathroom.

Originally, many Sheetrock walls and vanilla ceilings threatened the vibe of this log cabin. So we designed a fabric in a patchwork quilt pattern to use as a wall covering in the enormous entrance hall. Instead of staining the wood ceilings to match the walls, we decided that all the wood planks should be painted that wonderful shade of gray-blue the sky turns on a snowy day. And then to heighten the fantasy, we stenciled snowflakes on the ceiling. One reason we could go out on a limb with tongue-in-cheek touches on this project is that nothing we did inside could ever overwhelm the breathtaking views of the surrounding countryside, which is peaceful and majestic. 🏠

RIGHT The design of the hooked and braided oval rug in the foyer is from a drawing by Adam Lowenbein of the state of Idaho and some of its tourist attractions. Jan Jurta did the braiding.

OPPOSITE The felicitous relationship between Pop and folk art comes together in the design of the Robert Indiana–inspired fabric and pillows made by Sara Bruce for the seating in the living room.

FAR RIGHT The thirteen-foot-high totem poles were made in Minnesota and then shipped to New York so that they could be painted in coordinating colors.

RIGHT AND BELOW RIGHT In the sitting room of the master bedroom, the striped upholstery is a counterpoint to the hooked and braided rug that includes fanciful versions of vintage motel signs.

ABOVE LEFT, ABOVE, AND OPPOSITE
Three chests demonstrate the pairing of
old and new rustic pieces, the key to the
house's decor. One of a set, above left,
the blue chest with horn pulls by
Anthony Baratta was made in New York
for this house; the large, more elegant
chest, above, is an Austrian antique that
looks right at home in the American log
house; and the cottage-style cabinet,
opposite, with its painted landscape, is
an antique that now sits in one of the
guest bedrooms.

LEFT AND OPPOSITE
The rug in the upstairs
sitting room is patterned
with birch picture frames
and the Airstreams that
dot the property and function as extra guest rooms
in the summer months.
The open area is a cool
place to hang out. All
the fabrics were custom-
designed for this room.

RIGHT The Adirondack-style king-size bed in the master bedroom was crafted by Paul Flammang and features scenes from American national parks painted by Eric Beare. Above it hangs an over-scale vintage sign.

LEFT In the upstairs game room, the television is hidden in a custom-made cabinet covered in birch bark and hickory twigs.

LEFT The children's bathroom has four sinks and four sets of doors that open to reveal medicine cabinets and linen closets. All are painted with Idaho scenes depicting the different seasons. The counters are made of fire-engine red Corian.

OPPOSTE The bunk room has been out-fitted with eight beds and is one of the favorite rooms in the house for the three girls who live there. A tiny vintage fabric remnant inspired the pattern of the rug, which was hooked for the room by Stark Carpet and carried out in shades of green and blue. The designers had snowflakes stenciled on the wood ceiling to give the house a slight Nordic air.

NAUTICAL *Because the house on Cape Cod, a 1930s summer cottage, would be our second project for this charming couple, we already had an established comfort level with them. We understood their color preferences and her desire for everything to be happy and fun. They encouraged our creativity to show through, and even though we had only a few months to do the work, they were able to enjoy the house the following summer. We developed the decor by using pastel colors and lots of detailing based on seaside motifs such as windmills, sailboats, shells, and summer flowers.*

OPPOSITE Diamond Baratta Design added the porch to give the Cape Cod house a more charming and regionally authentic look. The settle, one of a pair that frames the front door, has cutouts of windmills that match those on the shutters. The nineteenth-century coach lantern, one of two on either side of the door, is among the largest the designers had ever seen.

RIGHT The lighthouse-shaped newel post with an illuminated beacon, the mahogany trim featuring carved wood stars, and the floor stained in a compass design are nautical details the designers brought to the summerhouse. A painted pink ceiling provides a "sweet and unexpected" finish, Bill says.

LEFT Hyport Regatta, a Lee Jofa by Diamond Baratta Design fabric with a sailboat motif, has been used on the deep sofas and Orkney chairs in the family room. Remnants of star quilts and antique hooked rugs have been made into pillows. The mahogany tables, crafted from old portholes and trimmed in brass, add another boatlike detail.

BELOW LEFT The designers created the Diamond and Roses fabric for Lee Jofa, which is used for the large sofa in the pastel-toned living room. An antique marine trunk serves as a coffee table. Window shades in a mattress-ticking-style fabric and the checkered rug keep the room from getting too sweet. The lamps' bases are made from large tole vases.

OPPOSITE Overlooking the water, the trellised room is one of the most pleasant places to pass the time. Nautical motifs are incorporated into the wood lattice, adding to the whimsy of the space. Diamond Baratta Design affixed mahogany arms to the couch based on American decorator Sister Parish's favorite Aiken sofa.

LEFT For one of the children's rooms, the designers devised a bed in the shape of a boat and added bedside tables that look as though they were plucked from a nearby pier.

OPPOSITE Details of the motifs on the painted floors and the custom-made cutouts—all of summery seaside elements, from flip-flops to anchors—add a layer of richness and fun to the house.

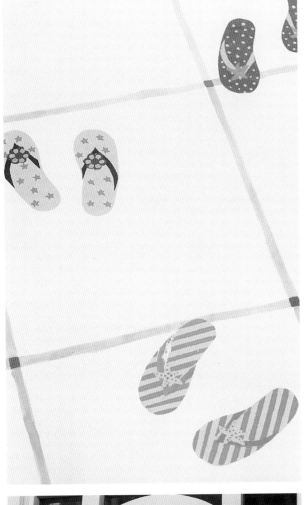

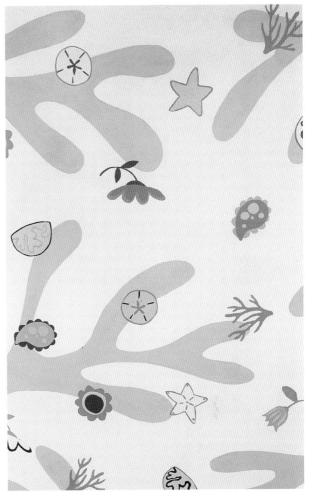

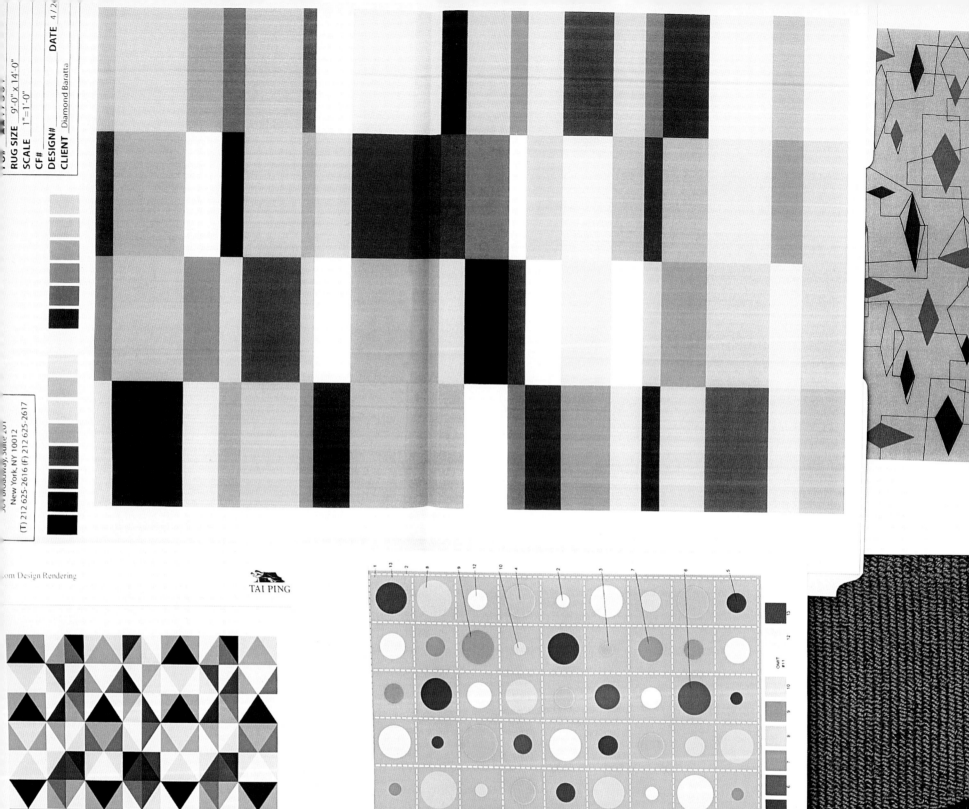

RUG SIZE 9'-0" x 14'-0"
SCALE 1" = 1'-0"
CF#
DESIGN#
CLIENT Diamond Baratta
DATE 4/2

New York, NY 10012
(T) 212 625-2616 (F) 212 625-2617

...om Design Rendering

TAI PING

1 2 3 4 5 6 7 8

Project Number DH50870
Design Number GH00359-1
Repeat Size 168.0" x 206.0"
Repeats Shown
Scale 1/2" = 1'
Quality 10/10
Date 4/11/2006 10:00:40 AM
Designer MS

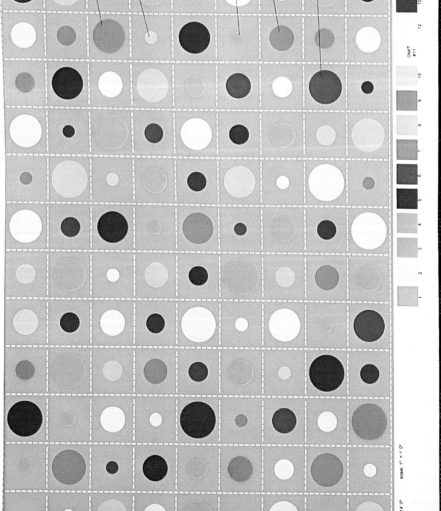

M O D

Diamond Baratta Design has redefined the contemporary interior. Bold colors, inventive fabrics, and graphic rugs once again take center stage—at the beach, in the city, or in the suburbs. Drawing on the psychedelic sixties and the avant-garde seventies and adding tasty bits from the thirties, forties, and fifties, as well as Pop Art, Tony and Bill have honed their modernist style. Rich with references, and far from minimalistic, it is totally original.

LEFT A collage of rug patterns inspired by the fifties and sixties is a stepping-off point for a new scheme.

BEACHY *When these clients called with the news of finally having found the perfect weekend house a stone's throw from the ocean, we were thrilled because we had had a lot of fun working on the family's Manhattan townhouse (which was used as the home of Meryl Streep's character in the movie The Devil Wears Prada). Although our clients' new house was a neo-traditional, shingle-style "cottage," they wanted a modern interior. They didn't want it to be serious or severe; they wanted an easygoing house—a place to hang out in with their kids and friends. The palette they chose could not have been simpler or beachier: blue and sand.*

The project was a breeze—or more precisely, a whirlwind. Even though our vision was crystal clear, the clients gave us a short period of time to execute it because they

wanted to move in for the summer. The foyer was easy: We designed it around a stunning Enoc Perez painting of the United Nations Headquarters; the piece hangs across from a 1970s Cubist mirror and a white console painted blue inside. The dining room was more of a challenge, since its primary window faces the driveway. To give this uninteresting room a new point of view, we installed a custom photomural of the ocean on three walls and designed a white-and-beige braided rug that looks like raked sand. This is definitely a house for barefoot living.

When we planned the living room, we had no idea that the clients would hang a Frank Stella painting over the sofa. But the painting looks sensational paired with a custom-made geometric rug inspired by one of the avant-garde Italian architect

Gio Ponti's patterns. And nothing quite compares to the museum-quality Alex Katz painting of a woman on the beach— it looks fantastic against the blue walls. (We've never understood why people think great art deserves white walls.) This must be the bluest house we have ever done, though it's safe to say that blue is our clients' favorite color. And you know what? We get it. Blue rooms are ethereal and heavenly. 🏠

ABOVE LEFT Inside the newly built but traditional shingle-style house are many vignettes that place the interior squarely in the twenty-first century. Near the front door, a surfboard by Christopher Makos hangs above a wavy vinyl bench by Diamond Baratta Design. The rug was inspired by a sixties textile.

ABOVE The faceted mirror in the hall came from Mondo Cane, a shop in Manhattan. The custom-made console has a white lacquered exterior and a blue interior.

ABOVE The stairway and a painting of the United Nations Headquarters by Enoc Perez can be glimpsed from the dining room.

ABOVE On the first-floor landing, an architectural photograph creates a dramatic counterpoint to the paneled walls.

LEFT In the library, the glass and walnut coffee table allows a view of the carpet, whose pattern was inspired by a textile from the English designer Lucienne Day.

OPPOSITE The dining room's wraparound photomural of waves at the shore makes it the most dramatic space in the house. The Brazilian walnut table, with its white lacquered base, sits on a circular, pale beige-and-white braided rug that is meant to recall the raked sand patterns of a Japanese Zen garden. The chairs, by Diamond Baratta Design, recall a model from the sixties. The sparkling crystal chandelier was made in Paris.

LEFT Tile patterns by Ponti inspired the look but not the scale of the geometric rug in the living room. The doughnut-shaped ottomans are by Diamond Baratta Design. On the wall above the early-1960s-style sofa is a 1968 acrylic painting, *Protractor Variation Xiii,* by the renowned American artist Frank Stella. Marilyn Henrion created the patchwork pillows.

LEFT On the other side of the living room, *Ada's Morning,* painted in 2000 by the American Pop artist Alex Katz, hangs near a late-1950s-style sofa. The lamp was made from a fiberglass plant stand that came from the Conran Shop in New York. The tables were bought at a flea market in London.

OPPOSITE A marble-topped table for Knoll by the Finnish architect Eero Saarinen is surrounded by a series of French designer Philippe Starck's Emeco chairs, which have been powder-coated in blue.

ABOVE In the blue-and-white guest room, the mirrored bedside table adds a touch of Hollywood glamour.

ABOVE A chair by Ponti is in the sitting area of the master bedroom. The draperies were custom-made for the room with a border in the classic Greek wavelike motif called running dog.

RIGHT The circular rug in the master bathroom was custom-designed and, along with the graphic wallpaper, updates the room's traditional bones with a contemporary look.

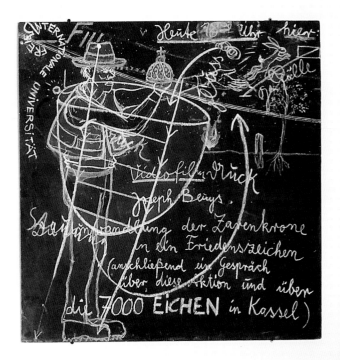

HANDSOME *If you thought you could move right in to a multimillion-dollar apartment on Central Park West, into a brand-new building designed by a world-renowned architect in the tradition of Manhattan's great prewar buildings, you would be wrong. When our client first showed us his apartment—which has the most gorgeous, most romantic treetop views of the park—we were, frankly, stumped about what to do with it. What's more, he had already settled on the intriguing color scheme of orange and green— and even though we understood that the colors related to the trees in the park, the palette was challenging nonetheless.*

To create a focal point and a sense of balance in the open living and dining areas, we installed a stainless-steel and limestone mantel in the middle of the wall, allowing room for two banquettes.

The client insisted the apartment have a unique look that could not be classified as either modern or contemporary. He wanted the apartment to have a timeless quality. He also wanted a paneled library, and he specified the color and texture of the wood. We used a light figured anegre that was just right for his apartment. We appreciate clients who engage and enlighten us; they remind us that the decorator is not always right! 🏠

LEFT To give definition to the large but unstructured living room, Bill and Tony added a 1930s-style faux fireplace and edged its asymmetrical hearth with a strip of stainless steel. The alterations were appropriate because decorative fireplaces are commonplace in prewar apartments, and the modern-day version of a Manhattan archetype extends the spirit of the building. On either side of the mantel, the designers built banquettes, which turned out to be the best solution for the space since they provide for separate dining and living areas. The banquettes are covered in Tango, a Lee Jofa burnt orange, raised-pinwheel chenille fabric by Diamond Baratta Design. The leather on the dining room chairs was matched in the exact same color. The rug has autumnal hues mixed with grays. The art includes, from left, *Carole*, a painting by Enoc Perez; *Femme*, a sculpture by Joan Miró; *Campbell's Soup Box Top 10.011*, a drawing by Andy Warhol; and one from the series *About a Bicycle* by Joseph Beuys.

LEFT It took twenty sketches before the client was satisfied with the credenza for the foyer—a glass-paneled, lacquered cabinet that now sits against an espresso-colored wall. The cabinet has been fitted with lacquered ovals; the hardware, a series of small stars, was made for the piece. Italian sconces from the 1950s frame the custom-made Diamond Baratta Design orange-glass-framed mirror.

RIGHT Bouquets of gerbera daisies stand out against the two-tone quilted pillows on the banquette. The set of Indian marquetry boxes is in the same colors as the living room.

LEFT In the living room, the Diamond Baratta Design parchment cabinet, created specially for the client and housing a mirror-lined bar, looks as though it could have been made in the 1930s—or the 1970s.

RIGHT Two leather-covered dining chairs frame Tom Friedman's *Tall Small Figure*, made in 2008. The client bought the sculpture and had it delivered on moving-in day.

LEFT AND OPPOSITE Art monographs are neatly stacked on the shelves of the *anegre*-wood-paneled library, built by Tony Wala, which overlooks Central Park. The light tan African wood was finished with a high-gloss lacquer to give the room the feeling of a luxurious, modern cigar humidor. The upholstery is a handwoven moss green chenille, with pillows in a checkerboard fabric created for this project. A large leather ottoman doubles as a coffee table. The two-dimensional rug is from Diamond Baratta Design for Stark Carpet, and the door panels leading to the kitchen are made of patterned glass. The sofa arm was also crafted from *anegre,* and the steel legs were inspired by the work of the German architect Mies van der Rohe.

LEFT AND OPPOSITE The kitchen was expanded to make room for a table by Eero Saarinen for Knoll and four white-leather-covered chairs by Le Corbusier from Cassina. The counters are made of lava stone; the backsplashes are green reverse-painted glass. The walls are lined in *anegre* to match the adjacent library.

ARTY *When we work on new houses, we like to be part of the construction process so that we can add (or subtract) architectural details to ensure that form reinforces function. But in the case of this McMansion in suburban Connecticut, we were too late. Our clients bought this uptight, 16,000-square-foot house from a builder (and we think they downplayed the size—it's ginormous). Although luxurious by conventional standards, the house was the most traditional, symmetrical, boring, and pretentious place we had ever seen. Columns were everywhere, as were dadoes, chair rails, and elaborate mantelpieces. The owners are modernists who collect contemporary art, and they wanted the house to be colorful and reflect a creative, anything-goes spirit.*

Conceptually, we approached the house like a painting: We used blocks of color to organize space. The foyer, which has a classical, sweeping banister, sets the tone. The two-story stair hall was turned into a site-specific artwork by the acclaimed Austrian artist Otto Zitko. In an alcove opposite the stairs, we installed a do-it-yourself piece, created by Olaf Nicolai, that is vibrant, unexpected, and fulfills the clients' desire for a house that looks like no one else's. To further underscore the art theme, we designed custom rugs throughout, using as inspiration the works of artists such as Richard Diebenkorn, Franz Kline, and Cy Twombly.

Because the man in the family is a serious chef, the kitchen is the most important room in the house. And this may be the most original, most spectacular kitchen we've ever designed. The Sub-Zero refrigerators are hidden behind panels of reverse-painted glass that look like Pop Art versions of a paint store's color strips. Our out-of-the-box thinking extended to the dining room, where we had two tables designed with sculptural bases that look like pickup sticks. One table is square, the other is round, and even though this dining room clearly works for groups of eight or sixteen, it can also seat twenty-four. The round table splits into half-moons that can be connected with leaves to either end of the square table. Throughout this house, surprises are the norm, and functionality is synonymous with artistry. It's really a modern house in a traditional shell. 🏠

PREVIOUS PAGES Beautifully sited on a slight rise near a suburban Connecticut town, the stone and wood columned house is huge and sprawling with a pair of symmetrical wings built onto the three-story main structure. Bought by a dynamic couple who have two young children, the exterior presents a rather traditional, low-key presence. The interiors, on the other hand, celebrate not only the clients' taste for contemporary art but also the designers' willingness to go beyond already charted decorating expressions.

OPPOSITE On the ground floor, strips of brightly colored paper—from a kit by artist Olaf Nicolai—line the curved foyer, where an eleven-foot-long sofa with portholes by Diamond Baratta Design was customized to fit the space. The high-backed chair is by Gio Ponti, the Italian architect and designer. The rug is loosely inspired by an early painting by Frank Stella, the American artist.

RIGHT Bill and Tony wanted to do something they describe as amazing on the walls around the swirling main staircase, so the clients commissioned the Austrian artist Otto Zitko to create a free-form mural that would be both eye-catching and memorable.

LEFT Throughout the house, the walls are painted a warm gray, with the doorframes and other woodwork painted in white. Long hallways necessitated special, dramatic floor treatments. On the ground floor, a fifty-foot-long runner recalls the work of Cy Twombly, the contemporary American artist known for his loose calligraphic images. Tony designed the circle-in-a-square lanterns.

RIGHT The runner by Stark Carpet on the second floor is about seventy feet long and has a border on one side with a design inspired by the Wiener Werkstätte, the early-twentieth-century movement in Austria. A drawing by Claes Oldenburg hangs at one end of the hallway.

ABOVE The living room is done in a palette of blue, red, and white, with vintage and iconic modern furniture pieces combined with some of Bill and Tony's designs. Hand-looped in China, the large rug is reminiscent of the fluid brushstrokes of the California painter Richard Diebenkorn. The chaise longue is a Harvey Probber design from the 1970s.

Adding to the mix of periods is the suite of Art Deco furniture, centered by the windows, which has been reupholstered in a handwoven, basket-patterned suede. The pillows are needlepoint versions of paintings by Sonia Delaunay and Frank Stella. Between the windows hangs a 2001 monotype by Richard Serra, the American sculptor.

ABOVE Cerulean blue lacquered walls and a rug patterned loosely on a work by Adolph Gottlieb, the American Expressionist painter, define the music room. The custom-made curvy sofa is a Diamond Baratta Design based on models from the 1950s. The photographic print on the left is a 2007 piece by London-based artist Idris Kahn; the 1991 etching on the wall is by contemporary American artist Brice Marden.

LEFT The game room is furnished with chairs that the American designer Warren Platner created for Knoll in the late 1960s. The vintage table is by Giuseppe Terragni, the Italian architect who died in 1943.

OPPOSITE The zebra pattern on the low pull-up chairs is printed on horsehair. A lively graphic statement is made with a chair arranged against the rug and a Fornasetti plate on one of the Italian blue glass nesting tables.

ABOVE The large dining room has been set up for maximum flexibility, for entertaining on a small or large scale. The overall design plays on the theme of the circle and the square. Two tables, one round, one square, have been positioned under two French crystal chandeliers, one round, one square, but can be joined to seat up to twenty-four people. The painting is by the German artist Gerhard Richter.

ABOVE Slim open-backed chairs, lacquered in white, contribute to the feeling of airiness in the room. They are light enough to be moved around easily when the configuration of the tables is changed.

ABOVE The long wood sideboard, outfitted with cutlery drawers, is an original design by Gio Ponti. Pakistan-born artist Shazia Sikander's 2002 series of lithographs, *No Parking Anytime*, stretches across the wall. Pieces of vintage glass add notes of color.

OVERLEAF The huge stainless-steel kitchen is the center of activity in the house. Blue glass reverse-painted panels are set into a grid of white aluminum. The color of the glass, in a seven-step gradation, transforms the wall into a work of conceptual art while disguising four full-size Sub-Zero refrigerators and eight freezer drawers. The panels could not be more practical for a kitchen, since they can be cleaned with Windex. Two islands—one with a hose faucet, the other in a racetrack shape—have counter surfaces impervious to heat. The large industrial-looking light fixtures are from Urban Archaeology in New York.

OPPOSITE AND RIGHT Just off the kitchen is the breakfast room, whose floor is covered in a braided rug made up of a series of two squares sewn together. The squares' yin and yang design has yellow, orange, and blue elements. The colors are echoed in the grid of the tabletop, inspired by a Gio Ponti design. Aluminum chairs designed by Philippe Starck for Emeco have been powder-coated in orange.

OPPOSITE A vintage Ponti chair, lacquered in blue and upholstered in channeled blue and white terrycloth fabric, is reflected in the mirror of the master bathroom. Adam Lowenbein painted the floor in a design that recalls a Ponti tile pattern.

ABOVE The spacious master bedroom suite is decorated in blue and white and includes a sitting area with a nickel-plated mirror. Draperies are edged in an embroidered, ribbonlike trim reminiscent of designs from the Wiener Werkstätte.

ABOVE A wall of reverse-painted glass in blue and white stripes lines the fireplace.

OVERLEAF In the master bedroom, the designers had a niche carved out of the wall in which to center the bed. The headboard of upholstered circles was inspired by the Marshmallow sofa by American designer George Nelson. The painted bedside tables were made for the room by craftsman Juan Sierra, and the fabric was designed for this bed. Louise Bourgeois, the Paris-born artist who is now in her late nineties, created La Reparation, a series of seven engravings, in 2003.

ABOVE Situated in another wing of the house, the spacious guest suite is a study in intense orange. The Lucite coffee table and the yellow wall cabinet add to the room's seventies aura. The geometric carpeting is by Diamond Baratta Design for Stark Carpet. The bedspread and sofa are covered in a Diamond Baratta Design fabric of interlocking lozenge-shaped pills.

ABOVE AND ABOVE RIGHT The guest
bathrooms are rendered in vibrantly
colored reverse-painted glass: One
bathroom, in shades of orange, is
situated near the children's playroom
in the basement; the other, in a range
of blues, is near the tasting room, with
its bright blue–skyed vineyard scene.

ABOVE The adjacent wine cellar, with its cerused oak cabinetry, holds an enviable collection of wine. A window offers a view onto the faux scenery.

RIGHT In the wine-tasting room, photographs by Sara Matthews, from her book *Washington: The State of Wine,* have been made into floor-to-ceiling murals.

TAILORED *We often feel more like doctors than decorators—especially when asked to perform emergency surgery on a house that is already under construction. We got a call one day from Frank Mori, a lovely gentleman who was building a new home next door to the country club where he was the president, in Bridgehampton, New York. He had been to one of our client's houses, and he loved our style—but we told him we couldn't work for him unless he was willing to halt construction, because the layout was all wrong. We've learned from experience that if you want a house decorated by Diamond Baratta Design, then you have to have Diamond Baratta Design architecture, too.*

After working with the architect, we were able to make adjustments to the interior. We opened it up, creating a barnlike loft that would suit the client's request for a low-key version of our bold style using a clean, simple palette. The stone chimneys had already been built, so we opted for complementary wood floors and white plank walls, which is often our coping mechanism when confronted with Sheetrock.

The clients were very clear that they abhorred clutter. Although they did not want extraneous accessories or decorative objects, they did want an undercurrent of excitement and a dash of brio. The hooked rug is a patchwork of alternating concentric squares in a range of blues, and the lacquered coffee table is a dark blue, the exact same shade as a navy Bentley. The repetition of blues in geometric sequences became this home's leitmotif, which is even included in the large open kitchen's backsplash. 🏠

PREVIOUS PAGES The second-floor balcony offers a bird's-eye view of the main sitting area and its striking stone fireplace. The materials for the interior were kept very simple, and a limited palette was chosen for the entire house. An open kitchen, convenient to the informal dining area that looks onto the fields at the back, was once an open porch. The overscale coffee table by Ron Seff is lacquered in dark blue. The hooked rug is a series of concentric squares in a range of blues; it combines a feeling of country style with an urban sophistication. Chairs in the style of French designer Jean-Michel Frank are covered in fabric that recalls traditional horse blankets the designers saw in a book on the couturier Cristobal Balenciaga.

OPPOSITE The custom-designed club chairs, trimmed in leather, are a nod to the house's setting, which adjoins a gracious horse farm. The director's chairs have oak frames, leather slings, and checked fabric backs.

ABOVE Opposite the kitchen are a second seating area and a more formal dining area, where woven-back chairs from Scotland's Orkney Islands have been reconfigured to dining height.

OPPOSITE A blue-and-gray color scheme permeates the home's interior. In the stairwell, a clock lantern designed by Tony and made by Charles Edwards in London hangs dramatically in front of a modern tapestry by Marilyn Henrion, a New York artist who reinterprets the geometry of Amish quilts.

RIGHT Country Floors, in New York, made the glazed ceramic tiles for the kitchen backsplash in a range of blues; the simple yet functional space is convenient to both dining areas.

BELOW RIGHT In the den, the specially made armoire by Paul Flammang hides a television and has a compass crafted from veneers in the manner of traditional marquetry. The room's nautical air is emphasized by the model ships.

ABOVE AND OPPOSITE The patterns of
four hooked rugs—geometric, basket
weave, patchwork, and concentric
squares—display some of Diamond Baratta
Design's favorite decorating motifs and
enliven the different spaces of the house.

TROPICAL "Anything *is possible when it comes to interior design*" is the philosophy of the couple who built this waterfront house on the Gulf of Mexico. Previously, they had done a lot of decorating, working with us and other designers. Fortunately, this couple has the passion and the interest to push boundaries, and their enthusiasm pushed us: They were willing to take risks, and so were we.

They wanted the home's interiors to be as vivid and tropical as its exterior. As so often happens, we started with a big white box, even though this one had some exquisite architectural details such as stunning windows. We bought a zillion yards of turquoise linen to cover many of the walls—and that was just the starting point!

We were encouraged to turn up the volume, which led to many bold moves that included the three-story stairwell mural inspired by Paul Gauguin and the hand-carved trellis-and-mirror dining room. For the family room, we upholstered the wicker as if it were English Chesterfield furniture, using Hawaiian prints custom-colored in green and turquoise. And we designed a rug that is a madcap mixed metaphor: a jungle of paisley gone insane. These major productions were planned to the nth degree, and we obsessed over every detail. This house is the quintessence of custom decorating— a personal reflection of the owners' sensibilities—and we had fun reinterpreting familiar themes for the couple. 🏠

OPPOSITE The intense light of the tropical landscape inspired not only the turquoise on the exterior but also the vividly colored interiors.

ABOVE LEFT The Venetian glass chandelier and the walls covered in yards of Scalamandré fabric turn up the volume in the front hall.

ABOVE The South Sea Islands mural by Eric Beare and the custom stair runner by Stark Carpet, edged in a pattern of sea crests, create a one-of-a-kind fantasy in the stairwell.

ABOVE White accents were used in the family room to set off the green and turquoise fabrics from Raoul Textiles that were custom-colored for the house. The artwork is by photographer Wendy Vroom, who specializes in vibrant close-ups of flowers.

ABOVE The living room, with its spectacular view of the Gulf of Mexico, has a
white lacquered coffee table surrounded
by armchairs with black lacquered wood
frames incised in a silver-leaf motif.

Needlepoint pillows of tropical blooms—
all designed for this house—stand out on
the white-piping-edged sofa covered in a
fabric from Brunschwig & Fils.

OPPOSITE Originally installed in a 1960s hotel, Venetian glass lighting fixtures from Salviati are clustered over the island in the kitchen. Its counters are topped with lava stone in a chartreuse color. The English sycamore wood island cabinets have been given a high-gloss finish and bands of polished nickel. Door knockers turned into handles are set into reverse-painted glass panels.

RIGHT The breakfast room plays on a design of circles, squares, and swirls. Lacquered wood balls decorate the fanciful chandelier. A table made for the room by Gregory Gurfein Woodwork sits on a rug that recalls Emilio Pucci's designs from the psychedelic sixties.

LEFT The custom-designed bed is set into a velvet niche and has a matching headboard; the patchwork pillows are by Erin Wilson; the luxurious, hand-sewn scalloped sheets are by Schweitzer.

RIGHT The floor in the master bedroom is covered with a Diamond Baratta Design carpet from Stark, on which tropical flowers such as hibiscus, allamanda, and passionflower are encircled by trellis-like bamboo frames.

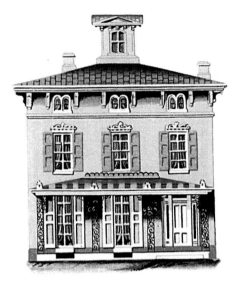

Adams, Rebecca Knapp. "The Eyes Have It." *House Beautiful,* March 2005, 92–99.

Albrecht, Donald, Ellen Lupton, Mitchell Owens, and Susan Yelavich. *Inside Design Now: National Design Triennial.* New York: Princeton Architectural Press, 2003.

Assouline. *Inspired Styles.* New York: Assouline, 2007.

Banks, Jeffrey, Doria de La Chapelle, and Rose Marie Bravo. *Tartan: Romancing the Plaid.* New York: Rizzoli, 2007.

Barreneche, Raul A. "Their Own Private Idaho." *Western Interiors,* January/February 2004, 106–117.

Bennetts, Leslie. "By the Seaside, Old-fashioned Charm." *The New York Times,* July 30, 1987.

Book, Jeff. "In Living Color." *Coastal Living,* June 2006, 144–149.

Campbell, Marina Isola. "Camp Baratta." *Hamptons Cottages & Gardens,* August 1–15, 2002.

Cerio, Gregory. "Honey, I'm Home." *House & Garden,* April 2001, 170–179.

Chevron, Doris. "Tony's Toyshop." *Architectural Digest* (Germany), July/August 2005, 128–135.

Colman, David. "A Place to Park the Imagination." *The New York Times,* February 18, 2007.

———. "Rhapsody in Blue." *Elle Decor,* May 2006, 174–181.

———. "Tilting Tradition with Punch-Line Proportions." *The New York Times,* February 12, 2004.

Dell'Aquilo, Bobbie. "Mutual Admiration." *New York Home,* March/April 2006, 74–81.

De Lorenzo, Cristiano. "Folie turquoise." *Case da abitare,* March 2008, 118–125.

Diamond, William, Anthony Baratta, and Dan Shaw. *Diamond Baratta Design.* New York: Bulfinch, 2006.

DiPiero, Diane. "A Colonial … Revolution." *Classic American Home,* February/March 2001, 38–45.

———. "Adamant Choice." *Classic American Home,* November 2001, 54–61.

———. "2001: A Space Odyssey for the Kitchen." *Classic American Home,* February/March 2001, 82–84.

Donelson, Sophie. "Canvassing the House." *Hamptons Cottages & Gardens,* August 15–31, 2008, 76–81.

Drucker, Stephen. "Summer Camp on Long Island." *Architectural Digest,* July 1994, 140–146.

Dunlop, Beth. "Blue Floride." *Architectural Digest,* April 2009, 146–151.

———. "Upbeat Blues." *House & Garden,* July 2007, 62–69.

Gaynor, Elizabeth. "Whimsy by the Sea." *Veranda,* June 2008, 200–213.

Gelpke, Anne. "Life Is a Beach." *Residence,* June 6, 2008, 48–56.

Grace, Lygenia. "Combine and Conquer." *House & Garden,* October 2002, 164–176.

Greene, Elaine. "The Country Set." *House & Garden,* December 1987, 162–169.

———. "Engaging Eccentricity." *House & Garden,* November 1986, 218–225.

———. "New American Mix." *House Beautiful,* February 1986, 56–63.

———. "New Frontier." *House Beautiful,* November 1988, 75–79.

———. "Perfectionists at Play." *House Beautiful,* April 2000, 106–113.

———. "Relaxing the Rules." *House Beautiful,* January 1987, 39–46.

———. "Summery Blues." *House Beautiful,* August 1988, 51–55.

———. "The Value of the Best." *House Beautiful,* July 1984, 72–77.

Hamilton, William L. "House Proud; My Son, the Decorator." *The New York Times,* May 14, 1998.

Hamptons Cottages and Gardens. Hamptons Havens: The Best of "Hamptons Cottages and Gardens." New York: Bulfinch, 2005.

Harrell, Glenn. "Custom of the Country." *House & Garden,* August 1989, 116–121.

———. "Kitchen Magnetism." *House Beautiful,* (issue unknown), 80–83.

Henderson, Stephen. "North by Northeast." *Hamptons Cottages & Gardens,* September 2005, 98–105.

Henry, Sherrye. "Primary Motifs." *House & Garden,* August 1990, 80–87.

Hughes, Elizabeth Blish. "Gotham Gallic." *House & Garden,* June 2003, 96–105.

———. "Open House." *House & Garden,* May 2004, 132–139.

Hunter, Elizabeth H. "Dynamic Duo." *House Beautiful,* May 2001, 108–113.

———. "The Heart of the Home." *House Beautiful,* August 1989, 70–73.

Iovine, Julie V. "For Kids' Rooms, Bunnies Are Out, Biedermeier Is In." *The New York Times,* February 12, 1998.

———. "Harlequin Romance." *The New York Times,* April 2, 1995, 68–71.

———. "Houses-in-a-House for Young Patients." *The New York Times,* November 14, 1996.

———. "Minivan Makeovers: New Inside Looks for Soccer-Mom Mobiles." *The New York Times,* October 20, 1999.

Koch, Raimund. "Pop Decor." *House & Garden,* August 2001, 13–15.

Kron, Joan. "Welcome to the Fun House." *Home Style,* December 2001/January 2002, 44–55.

Kutlar, T. "Turkuaz Derinlik." *House Beautiful* (Turkey), April 4, 2005, 138–145.

———. "Ucantrenkler." *House Beautiful* (Turkey), August 2004, 100–109.

———. "Zevk Rastlantisal Degildir." *House Beautiful* (Turkey), June 6, 2006, 140–149.

Lee, Vinny. *Innovative Interiors: In Association with "The Times."* London: Pavilion, 2002.

Levinger, Martina. "Diamond Baratta." *Architectural Digest* (Germany), January 2008, 78–80.

Lima. "Florida Fantasy." *Deco Home* (Germany), June/July/August 2008, 56–63.

Loecke, John. "On the Waterfront." *Veranda,* July/August 2004, 96–107.

Loos, Ted. "Over the Top." *House Beautiful,* October 2003, 82, 118–127.

———. "Sense of Place." *Traditional Home,* April 2002, 124–131.

MacDougall, Frances and *Southern Accents. "Southern Accents" on Color.* New York: Bulfinch, 2003.

MacIsaac, Heather Smith. "The Insiders." *Elements of Living,* December 2005, 92, 96.

Manroe, Candace Ord. "Rocky Mountain High." *Traditional Home,* Holiday 2001, 92–101.

Margolies, Jane. "Folk Remedies." *House Beautiful,* March 2003, 92–103.

Marshall, Barbara. "Buoyant with Color." *Florida Design,* Vol. 9:2, 264–273.

Marx, Betsy. "Mutual Admiration." *New York Home,* March/April 2006, 74–81.

Marx, Linda. "Boca Rococo." *House Beautiful,* January 2003, 50–57.

Michael, Michele. *The New Apartment Book: Inspiring Ideas and Practical Projects for Decorating Your Home.* New York: Three Rivers Press, 1996.

Morant, Deborah. "Saturation Point." *Traditional Home,* May 2001, 169–181.

Nasatir, Judith. "Kap der Guten Launer." *Architectural Digest* (Germany), July/August 2003, 150–157.

———. "To the Light House." *House & Garden,* August 2002, 76–83.

Nicksin, Carole. "Cachet in the Attic." *The New York Times,* October 9, 2005, 54.

Oshin, Edith Sonn. "Victorian Plus." *House & Garden,* May 1983, 84–91.

Peters, Brooks. "Before and After: Building on Tradition." *Architectural Digest,* May 1995, 184–191.

Petkanas, Christopher. "Colorful Rooms … Colorful Kitchen." *House Beautiful,* May 2007, 96–105.

Pignatelli, Marina. "Allegri contrasti cromatic." *La mia casa,* April 2004, 106–113.

Pittel, Christine. "Eminent Victoria." *House & Garden,* May 1991, 124–131.

———. "Flying Colors." *House Beautiful,* July 2004, 90–98, 120.

———. "Pattern, Pattern, Pattern." *House Beautiful,* September 2006, 118–127.

Prisant, Carol. "Scintillating Diamond." *The World of Interiors,* January 1994, 49–57.

———. "Sunshine State." *The World of Interiors,* October 2008, 296–305.

Sacks, David. "Manhattan Country." *House & Garden,* April 1989, 132–143.

Schofield, De. "Expect the Unexpected." *Florida Design,* Vol. 18:2, 232–247.

Schultz, Frances. "Does Taste Have to Mean Safe?" *House Beautiful,* April 2006, 72–81.

———. "Relax." *Veranda,* July/August 2003, 130–135.

———. "Renewal." *Veranda,* July/August 2001, 114–227.

Shrady, Nicholas. "Country Life on Fifth Avenue." *Architectural Digest,* July 1996, 122–127.

Silva, Horacio. "London Calling." *The New York Times,* April 13, 2003.

Slesin, Suzanne. "Bold Effects, Country Style for a Weekend House." *The New York Times,* July 18, 1985.

———. "Up Country." *House & Garden,* April 2000, 160–167.

Solomon, Andrew. "Florida Fun House." *House & Garden,* May 1992, 102–107.

Somerville, Lydia. "Rhapsody in Blue." *Southern Accents,* May/June 2002, 176–185.

Szabo, Julia. "Color Up!" *House Beautiful,* April 2004, 134–139.

Tudor, Jason. "Twisted Tradition." *Connecticut Cottages & Gardens,* March 2005, 53–61.

Viladas, Pilar. "A Connecticut Yankee." *Architectural Digest,* November 1994, 218–225.

———. "Caesar's Other Palace." *The New York Times,* November 1, 1998, 58–61.

———. *Domesticities: At Home with "The New York Times Magazine."* New York: Bulfinch, 2005.

———. "Floats like a Butterfly." *The New York Times,* February 20, 2000, 51–56.

———. "Romper Rooms." *The New York Times,* September 21, 1997, 78–83.

———. "Schrage klassik." *Architectural Digest* (Germany), March 2007, 162–169.

———. "Tailor Made." *The New York Times,* June 18, 2006, 60–63.

Ward, Timothy Jack. "Closet Case." *Elle Decor,* February/March 2003, 140–147.

Whitcomb, Claire. "Go All the Way with Blue." *House Beautiful,* April 1987, 60–61.

Young, Lucie. "Truly, Madly, Deeply." *Traditional Home,* April 2004, 170–178.

We dedicate this book to our families and friends, for their unending support throughout our partnership.

We would like to acknowledge the many talented people who have helped to create this book: Suzanne Slesin, our leader, publisher, and longtime friend; Stafford Cliff, for his unique and unparalleled vision in designing the book; Michel Arnaud, for his magical photographs that make the projects come to life with the help of his assistant, Pawel Kaminski; Dan Shaw, whose brilliant writing is as inspiring as always; and Jane Creech, the managing editor, whose zealous work has made this whole experience so enjoyable. And to Jonathan Lazzara, Dominick Santise, and Regan Toews at Pointed Leaf Press—we are truly appreciative of all your hard work.

We are so proud of the involvement of the talented, hardworking team of Diamond Baratta Design and their tireless efforts in making our work become reality. Many thanks to Pamela Ackerman, Tom Ambler, Mauricio Bedoya, Melonie Edwards, Celi Jimenez, Angela Macias, Jaime Magoon, Kate McCabe, Evelyn Merine, Arian Myrto, Carlos Perez, Melissa Pinto, Rhiannon Price, and Kathryn Ungaro.

We would like to thank the editors and writers who have invited Diamond Baratta Design into the homes of their readers: D.J. Carey, Doris Chevron, David Colman, Stephen Drucker, Jason Kontos, Phyllis Lichtenstein, Lisa Newsom, Carol Prisant, Paige Rense, Margaret Russell, Anita Sarsidi, Doretta Sperduto, Newell Turner, Rupert Thomas, Pilar Viladas, and Michael Wollaeger.

We are greatly appreciative to Carmel & Robert Brantley, Tria Giovan, George Ross, and Jason Schmidt for the additional photography used in the book.

Diamond Baratta is proud of the work of the artists and artisans whom we have had the privilege of working with: Martha Baker, Eric Beare, the Bielecky family, Sara Bruce, Jimmy Cabrera, Steven Cavallo, Lois Chernin, David Cohn, Kevin Cross, Nicholas Didonato, Osmundo Echavaria, Paul Ferrante, Barry and Shelly Fienstein, Paul Flammang, Les Goss, Perry Guillot, Gregory Gurfein, Dora Helwig, Finn Hegner, Jan and Wayne Jurta, Kenneth Kayel and the DeAngelis family, Steve and Marjorie Klein, Bronko Kmet, Adam Lowenbein, Tom Newman, Michael Pell, Juli Pericak, Frank Pollaro, Jim and Dick Reeve, Tim Sheridan, Juan Sierra, Patricia Sullivan, Manny Theodosiou, Tony Wala, and May Yung.

We are also grateful to all the architects with whom we have collaborated on our many projects.

Thank you to the people who have helped deliver our creativity to the world: the Kravet family and Steven Elrod at Lee Jofa, and John Stark, Steven Stark, and Rick Zolt of Stark Carpet. Thank you also to Jill Cohen.

Finally, we cannot thank our clients and their families enough for allowing us into their homes and into their lives. We are so happy to have made their world a bit more joyful.

William Diamond and Anthony Baratta

New York City, April 2009

DUST JACKET FRONT For a zany sofa, and as a one-of-a-kind interpretation of the designs of Marimekko, Diamond Baratta Design had special needlepoint pillows made and thirty yards of the Finnish company's vintage fabric dyed in cobalt blue.

DUST JACKET BACK The foyer in William Diamond's house in East Hampton, New York, combines an antique Windsor bench with the cartoonlike painted floor.

COVER A sketch for a rug in a house on Captiva Island, Florida, was inspired by 1960s psychedelic graphics.

ENDPAPERS A sketch for pillows was inspired by a Gio Ponti tile design.

ENDPAPER VERSOS Diamond Baratta Design's Jensen wool rug for Stark Carpet has a pattern of circles.

OPPOSITE CONTENTS Nick Baratta, Tony's brother, photographed William Diamond and Anthony Baratta in 1991.

LEFT The cabinet in a boy's room is a riff on the work of American Pop artist Robert Indiana.

BELOW LEFT The chest in a girl's room is a feminine interpretation of the stacked drawer piece by Droog Design.

CREDITS

Unless noted, all images were either from the personal archives of the authors or photographed by Michel Arnaud on location with his assistant, Pawel Kaminski. Any omissions will be corrected in future printings. Acevedo/House & Garden © 2000 Condé Nast Publications, 22; Architectural Digest © 1994 Condé Nast Publications, 22; photography by Nick Baratta, 4; all photographs from the personal collection of Anthony Baratta, 14–15, 19, 25; Beuys © 2009 Artists Rights Society (ARS), New York/VG Bild-Kunst, Bonn, 153; Bootz/House & Garden © 2002 Condé Nast Publications, 23; art © Louise Bourgeois/licensed by VAGA, New York, NY, 180–181; photograph by Henry Bourne © The World of Interiors January 1994, 23; photography by Robert Brantley, Delray Beach, FL, courtesy Florida Design Inc., Boca Raton, FL, 194–199; all photographs from the personal collection of William Diamond, 10–12, 18, 24; courtesy of Florida Design Inc., Boca Raton, FL, 22, 23; photography by Tria Giovan, 76–81, 134–139; photography by Kari Haavisto, 20; © 2009 Damien Hirst, all rights reserved/ARS, New York/DACS, London, 52; reprinted by permission from House Beautiful, Hearst Communications Inc., all rights reserved, Jonn Coolidge, photographer (April 2000 cover), Tria Giovan, photographer (July 2004 and April 2005 covers), 22, 23; House & Garden © 2003 Condé Nast Publications, 23; photograph by Thibault Jeanson © The World of Interiors October 2008, 22; photography by Mark Jenkinson, 13; art © Alex Katz/licensed by VAGA, New York, NY, 148; © 2009 Successió Miró/Artists Rights Society (ARS), New York/ADAGP, Paris, 152; Mundy/House & Garden © 1990 Condé Nast Publications, 23; George Ross Photographs; photograph by Jason Schmidt, 16–17, 21, 23, 200–201; Schmidt/House & Garden © 2007 Condé Nast Publications, 22; photography by Thomas Hart Shelby, 6; © 2009 Frank Stella/Artists Rights Society (ARS), New York, 146; © 2009 the Andy Warhol Foundation for the Visual Arts/ARS, New York, 152.

136 Baxter Street, New York, NY 10013
www.pointedleafpress.com
Printed and bound in China.
First edition
10 9 8 7 6 5 4 3 2 1
Library of Congress Control Number: 2009924870
ISBN 10: 0-9823585-0-4
ISBN 13: 978-0-9823585-0-4